APPALACHIAN
R E V I E W

VOL. 51, NO. 3
SUMMER 2023

**50 YEARS OF
TRADITION. DIVERSITY. CHANGE.**

EDITOR
Jason Kyle Howard

BOOK REVIEWS EDITOR
Emily Masters

STUDENT ASSISTANTS
Lie Ford
Soul Nwaokoro
Ian Williamson

MANUSCRIPT READERS
Katherine Scott Crawford
Patti Frye Meredith

ADVISORY BOARD

Richard Hague
Marc Harshman
Maurice Manning
Karen Salyer McElmurray

Lee Smith
Lyrae Van Clief-Stefanon
Neela Vaswani
Crystal Wilkinson

ESTABLISHED IN 1973
PUBLISHED QUARTERLY
by Berea College
www.appalachianreview.net

Electronic submissions only at www.appalachianreview.net. Distributed through a partnership between the University of North Carolina Press and Duke University Press. Basic subscription price: $32/year for individuals, $62/year for institutions. For subscription requests and inquiries, visit the magazine's website, email subscriptions@dukepress.edu, or call 888-651-0122 (toll-free in the US and Canada) or 919-688-5134.

CONTENTS

INTERVIEW

BOOK REVIEWS

COVER PHOTOGRAPH
I wish you could smell this photograph by Carey Neal Gough

EDITOR'S NOTE

JASON KYLE HOWARD

There comes a point in Lindsey Pharr's essay "On Being Still and Knowing"—the lead piece of prose in this issue of *Appalachian Review*—where she muses about human nature. More specifically, where she recounts being "projected upon" and, in the process, subjected to all manner of abuse: just for being a woman with a voice, just for being a woman, just for being. "Projection," she observes, "is a vital ingredient of cruelty—it's a lot harder to treat someone badly if you actually see them as a human."

I've carried this thought with me over the past few weeks. I've considered how we have become increasingly conditioned to make dehumanizing projections through social media, which feels at once intimate and, because we are behind a keyboard, distant; through our celebrity culture, which often teaches us to view people as commodities rather than as fellow humans; and how it affects us on so many levels, including our politics, our work life and even our most intimate relationships.

But I've also thought of how literature and reading—how art—can point us toward a better way. Numerous studies have shown that reading builds empathy for others. It can narrow gaps of division and build bridges of understanding. "We tell each other stories in order to live," Joan Didion famously wrote in her essay "The White Album," and it strikes me that we also tell stories so as to better live with each other.

Consider this as you read the work in this issue. To accompany Pharr's essay, which is rooted in figure drawing and portraiture, we are proud to offer three poems by John Brooks. A visual artist and poet from Kentucky, his artwork has received national attention, most notably in a *New Yorker* essay by novelist Garth Greenwell, who praised Brooks's use of vivid color, the human figure, found images and homoeroticism to create what Greenwell called a "transhistorical community." Brooks is just as successful and captivating on the page. His poems sing with the language of hymnody, the natural world, loneliness, desire and the ache for human connection.

We are also pleased to publish a short story by Mindy Misener, an essay by Ashley Anderson, poems by Kate Wright, Tamara J. Madison, Garrett Stack and others, as well as a lively conversation between poets Ross Gay and Ansel Elkins.

In his conversation with Elkins, Gay offers the natural world as an antidote to "dehumanization." He lists soil, seeds, trees, critters, rain and sun as "real" elements worthy of our attention. And then he mentions something else: "Our relationships, and the deepening of them." May we all follow his and Pharr's calls to do better. To pay attention, to think twice, to recommit ourselves to making connections instead of projections. ■

2022 DENNY C. PLATTNER AWARDS

T he annual Plattner Awards were established in 1995 by Kenneth and Elissa Plattner to honor their late son and his love of writing. The awards are given to the finest pieces of fiction, creative nonfiction, and poetry that appeared in *Appalachian Review* during the previous year. Winners receive a $200 prize, and both winners and honorable mentions are awarded a handsome piece of handmade ceramics designed and manufactured by Berea College Crafts.

FICTION
Winner: Gavin Colton, "Little Piles of Change"
Honorable Mention: Christopher Labaza, "Kingsnake"

CREATIVE NONFICTION
Winner: Caroline McTeer, "Blue Ridge Bobby"
Honorable Mentions: Rachel Kesselman, "Where Do You Come From?" and Quincy Gray McMichael, "Grasping at Grace"

POETRY
Winner: Jeremy Paden, "Swimming"
Honorable Mention: Rita Mookerjee, "Half Ode to the Rope Swing I Never Climbed"

ON BEING STILL AND KNOWING

LINDSEY PHARR

The focal point of Jean-Léon Gérôme's painting *Pygmalion and Galatea* (1890) is, undeniably, Galatea's ass. It is this point on her body, just under those pert cheeks, to be exact, that her metamorphosis from cold white marble to warm, blushing flesh takes place. Standing on a platform in the middle of her creator's studio, the statue-woman's pose is full of tension, of muscular energy frozen in time. She leans over to kiss Pygmalion, who rises on his tiptoes to meet her. In the background floats an ephemeral Cupid on the brink of letting a love dart fly.

The myth of Pygmalion and Galatea goes like this: Pygmalion was a sculptor in Cyprus who, having no interest in living, breathing women, sculpted his ideal of one in ivory. He named his creation Galatea, meaning "milk-white woman." Pygmalion became enamored with his creation, bathing her, dressing her, bringing her trinkets, and gazing at her for hours. He prayed to Aphrodite to give him a woman just like the one he'd carved, and Aphrodite answered his prayer. Galatea came to life, she and Pygmalion had a daughter, and everyone lived happily ever after, as far as we know.

The story became a sort of obsession for Gérôme, who created at least five known versions in oil as well as a marble sculpture in the span of two years. Other versions show up in the backgrounds of his works *Working in Marble* (1890) and *The Artist and His Model* (1894)—two paintings that are almost exactly the same painting. Both self-portraits, they depict Gérôme in his studio at work on his sculpture *Tanagra* (1890) with his longtime model, Emma Dupont. On the wall behind the artist and his model hangs a rejected version of *Pygmalion and Galatea*, a more scandalous one that depicts the embrace complete with full frontal nudity. Alongside it in the artist's cluttered workshop stand examples of his other famous works. It's a bit dizzying, this lean towards the meta, a hall of fame of sorts within a painting about a sculpture. A painting about a myth about a sculpture whose creator's obsession brought her to life. A myth a that's unsettling to me, that feels a little like *The Velveteen Rabbit* meets *The Picture of Dorian Gray*. Gérôme seems to have never tired of gazing upon his own creations, of surrounding himself with them and revisiting them to make inexhaustible variations on a theme. It's easy to see the Pygmalion in him. He even signed the painting on the base of the sculpture of Galatea, his signature taking the place of Pygmalion's. The epitome of the male gaze, Pygmalion found himself under the obsessive eye of another male sculptor.

Looking more closely at Gérôme's *Pygmalion and Galatea*, other details come into focus. This studio is not Pygmalion's but Gèrôme's. *Selene*, one of his famous bronzes, sits on a shelf next to other sculptures. One depicts a woman in profile gazing into a hand mirror. Another is of two hooded figures, a woman and a child. The woman holds one hand to her mouth, while the other hand seems about to shove the child behind her to block its view of the lovers' embrace. A pair of theatrical masks, Tragedy and Comedy, hang on a wall. The aegis, Athena's shield, rests nearby. The shield's polished, mirror-like surface is adorned with Medusa's dead-eyed-but-dangerous stare. The objects gathered in the background of Pygmalion/Gèrôme's studio are about seeing and being seen. Mirrors and masks. I pointed out these details to a friend, my agitation rising as I struggled to articulate how the more I looked at the painting, the more it bothered me.

"Look again," I said. "Isn't Pygmalion's embrace a little, well, rough? Doesn't it look like Galatea's fingers are trying to pry his hand off her ribcage?"

"But he's the one reaching up to her," my friend counters. "She's literally above him, in a position of power. He's the supplicant here."

"But she's literally on a pedestal! She's not a real woman, she's his *ideal* of one!"

He cautiously suggested that I might be reading too much into the painting. I laughed and recalled an excerpt from Oscar Wilde's preface to *The Picture of Dorian Gray*: "Those who find ugly meanings in beautiful things are corrupt without being charming. This is a fault." Maybe I *am* reading too much into it. Or maybe I'm just so tired of being projected upon that I've started projecting back. I'm a typically quiet woman, which makes me *cold, aloof, intimidating.* When I was married and I spoke up in public, or God forbid, laugh too loudly, my husband would pinch my thigh under the table and hiss at me to "stop using my dyke voice." I've been called a whore for being the victim of sexual assault. Hell, I've been called a whore for smiling while wearing a sundress and having a nice day. Projection is a vital ingredient of cruelty—it's a lot harder to treat someone badly if you actually see them as a human.

While we can't see her face, the model for Galatea was almost certainly Emma Dupont. Imagine her on the modeling

Projection is a vital ingredient of cruelty—it's a lot harder to treat someone badly if you actually see them as a human.

stand in Gèrôme's drafty Parisian studio, her right arm encircling empty air where Pygmalion's shoulders would be, left hand pinning an imaginary palm to her breast, knees locked and trembling to counterbalance that lean into nothingness. I've held similar poses, ones in which an integral piece is missing. I've pretended to pour water, lift the lid of an imaginary box, reach toward an absent lover's face. Without thinking, I've settled into poses identical to Dupont's when she modeled for some of Gèrôme's most famous sculptures: *The Ball Player, Baccante with Grapes,* and *Corinth.* The classical art training I'd received prodigiously early in life left its mark so firmly that contrapposto became muscle memory.

I've worked as an artist's model for over a decade and a half. ("And your rates have never gone up!" laughed my friend who once worked full-time as a model for the huge animation studios in LA.) They haven't gone up because it's not exactly a bread-and-butter gig in this town, at least not anymore. This little mountain town used to be an artist's haven, but now very few artists can afford it. I have day jobs that pay the bills. I pose because I love it. Because it is mentally and physically challenging. Because I get to meet some very interesting people.

The only figure drawing an artist ever gave me—conté crayon, side view, reclining—my husband asked to keep when I moved out and has surely since thrown away. As the gray hairs come in and my backside bears increasingly less of a resemblance to that of Galatea, I find myself wishing I'd asked to keep a sketch or two over the years. For posterity.

Over the course of the twenty years that Emma Dupont modeled for Gèrôme, she must have seen her likeliness reproduced hundreds if not thousands of times. Here she is: a Greek athlete. Here an odalisque. Here an allegorical representation of Truth climbing out of a well. Imagine her standing before an army of Emily Duponts, face to face with the closest thing to immortality any of us could ever get. She arranges them chronologically, from ages seventeen to thirty-seven, and examines the differences. Did Gérôme make her forever young, or did he allow her likenesses to mirror the inevitable changes that the muse's body experiences? Did Emma Dupont keep any? Or was she like me, wishing she'd built a small collection for the sake of some nostalgic future self? In all her roleplaying for Gérôme's historical subjects, did Emma Dupont ever look at a painting of herself and feel *seen*?

The strictly Classical artistic tradition in which I was taught stressed the ability to translate what the eye sees onto the page as accurately as possible. Still life after still life, plaster bust after plaster bust, we learned to measure out proportions with our thumbs along the length of our pencils. We studied anatomy books and skeletons, closely examining how the human body built itself out layer by layer from its calcium frame. Live models were the ultimate test: not only was the anatomy in motion, but we had to capture the motion itself. Gesture sketches were part of our low-stakes warmup sessions. On cheap newsprint I tried to capture the movement of a pose as quickly as possible, often ripping the thin paper with my pencil's enthusiastic swoops and strokes. Contour drawings, the second part of our class warmups, were the most sensual of marks—following the topography of the figure's surface in one continuous line with a ball point pen, folds and joints became valleys and summits. At the time, it was the closest I could get to explaining how I saw my own body as an extension of the ground I stood on. It's the closest I can get now to describing love. The kind of love the poets seem to love best. That Pablo Neruda kind of love. The kind that delights in tracing the architecture of the beloved. The kind of love you feel when you lay your head on their chest and listen to their heartbeat as it chants *wonder, wonder, wonder.*

I remember nearly every model that I drew in those night classes. The first naked man I ever saw was on that modeling stand: a local sculptor who carved his poetry into cow bones with a Dremel tool. He kicked up into a one-armed handstand and held it for what felt like forever as the class scrambled to get down the topsy-turvy athleticism of the pose as quickly as possible. Except for me. Fourteen-years-old and frozen with my pencil in midair, I just didn't know where to look, so I drew his elbow as it strained to balance his weight. All of the models seemed incredibly glamorous and bohemian to my young eyes.

There was the gorgeous, head-wrapped Black woman with a rose tattooed on her thigh. The skinny white girl who had such luxurious pelts of soft fur under her arms that it looked like she had small animals nestled there. The deeply tanned mural painter who'd covered his Jeep bumper to bumper with stolen hood ornaments. The barrel-chested Zen monk. I wanted them to like the drawings I made of them so badly that, like an athlete under pressure, I choked.

The glide of pen over paper as I draft this essay feels almost as good as tracing a line along the contours of the body. It's taken me most of my adult life to reclaim the pleasure of making a mark. Back then, as classes intensified and my skill increased, the sensuality got hammered out and replaced by stress. I wasn't the only one who cracked under it. One night another student hit the end of his rope. He walked out after he flung a pencil across the room so hard it impaled a finished canvas hanging on the wall. We were taught that we had to get it *right*. And I couldn't get it right—or at least I thought I couldn't. I was unaware of the myriad ways in my life in which I could and would eventually fail. Looking back over my drawings from those days I can give myself some credit. They're really pretty good. The linework especially possesses an emotional quality, a lyricism. But the rigorous training I received became warped in my mind until I honestly believed that it was better to make no mark at all than to make an incorrect one. I couldn't stand the blank, accusing face of the empty page. So I stepped around to the other side of the easel.

There's a couple I've never met who have my portrait hanging in their Brooklyn apartment. Their first date took place at a tiny Italian restaurant in Oxford, Mississippi, where my portrait hung as part of a show. Years later the bride tracked down the artist and purchased it for her husband as an anniversary gift. I'm not sure why that painting specifically caught her eye. It probably had something to do with how the artist captured the rich red of the leather chair I was sprawled in, how its ruby glow matched the wine in their glasses. It's uncomfortable to think that it might have had something to do with the painting's subject: the impossibly young girl with the impossibly long legs. The one with the dreamy-sad face like a Mazzy Star song, who'd eventually leave her Ivy League painter for the town's biggest train wreck.

A few months ago, dug out an old shoebox from under the bed and found the reference photos that were taken for that painting. It's an experience we've all had, going through old photos and reminiscing, but it's a unique experience to look at a painting of yourself from the past. It's not quite you. It's an interpretation of you. There are three filters laid upon each other as you gaze into this mirror. Reality tilts, turns kaleidoscopic—the eyes you have now are looking through the eyes of someone you haven't spoken to in years who is looking upon a you that, in many ways, you no longer are. How did you get your hair to be that long? Why do you look so sad? Baby Girl, you've only just *met* the blues.

Before it hung in the tiny Italian restaurant, the painting hung in a tiny hometown gallery. At the packed opening, my high school art teacher shouted at me above the din, "Good Lord, child! Is that nekkid girl you?"

"No ma'am," I replied, pointing with the plastic cup of box wine that I was just now legally allowed to drink. "I'm over there."

She came to the opening because we had the same high school art teacher, the painter and I, and we both adored all four feet and ten inches of her. He, of course, had been one of her darlings. She had me stay behind after class one day and asked if I wanted to talk to the school chaplain—we didn't have a counselor—because my art seemed *disturbed*. This made me one of her darlings too, in a way.

In unconscious rebellion to the perfectionism of my night classes at the tiny studio downtown, I'd fallen in love with Basquiat and would spend my time in AP art class digging corrugated cardboard out of the trash behind the cafeteria to cover with oil-pastel imitations of his scrawled and angry brilliance. My early attempts at poetry marched along behind the figures, falling off one edge of the cardboard only to pop back up on the other side, a voice oblivious to any listener but desperate to be heard. There's another projection that often happens with quiet girls: people see them and think *well-mannered*. Teachers write comments like "a joy to have in class." Parents reassure themselves: *She's fine.* This teacher was the only one who saw how I stood on a precipice: a motherless child who'd never see the inside of a therapist's office until her thirties. A girl who'd fall, unseen, through a series of older men, desperately reaching for that handhold called love.

There are actually two portraits of me from the Italian restaurant art show. The one hanging in Brooklyn is nearly life-sized: I am sitting in a red leather armchair in my boyfriend-the-painter's blue Oxford button-down, legs stretched out towards the viewer, my dirty bare feet kicked up on an ottoman. The one hidden behind my father's bookshelf in a dusty corner of his office—the one given to me as a wedding present for my own doomed marriage that was so short-lived that the painting turned out to be more of a divorce present—is smaller. Same sad-eyed indie girl in a blue oxford button-down, same bare legs this time knees-up and folded into a blue and white striped chair.

"You look like a Jezebel," my stepmother says. Given the fact that I am fully covered, there's nothing overt about the painting that warrants her clicked tongue. My stepmother can be a surprisingly sensitive person, however. She's picking up on what he *didn't* paint: Early-morning sunlight. Crisp white sheets on a narrow bed. The smells of sleep and sex and laundry detergent. What it meant, exactly, for me to be wearing the shirt of this much older man.

We've all felt it, the biological phenomenon known as "gaze detection," that creepy sensation of feeling someone staring at you, of feeling every downy hair on the nape of your neck rise in alarm, the area we refer to in dogs as *hackles*. Now imagine standing naked on a platform in a studio—it's always chilly, the studio, wherever it may be—feeling several pairs of eyes staring

She's picking up on what he didn't paint: Early morning sunlight. Crisp white sheets on a narrow bed. The smells of sleep and sex and laundry detergent.

at you, causing goosebumps to rise wherever on your body a gaze lands. You discover that your entire body has hackles. You get used to it.

It works both ways, this vulnerability. While I might steal a glance out of the corner of my eye after I step down from the platform and wrap a bathrobe around me, and I might cast a passing glance over the easels on my way to the bathroom, I don't linger. I know better. Some artists turn their sketches over, cover them with a blank sheet of paper during the breaks. My friend who worked in the big animation studios is nothing if not charismatic. Like Emma Dupont, she often posed as characters: a Viking shieldmaiden, a psychedelic Alice, Marie Antoinette. A loud Italian with undeniable main-character energy, she did all her own makeup and costuming. She chatted with artists on her breaks, and her favorite sketches ended up on her social media feeds. My friend's future self, her potential children, maybe even grandchildren, will have plenty of proof of her glory days. I can only assume that they do things differently out in Hollywood, a place where everyone seems desperate to make their mark, to live forever in one form or another.

In Gèrôme's painting *The End of the Pose*, Emma Dupont throws a cloth over a sculpture of herself to protect it from dust while she herself remains nude, her glorious backside bare to the viewer while Gèrôme cleans his tools. The statue's face is already covered, as is the face of the tiny child tucked behind her. The statue is a clay maquette of Gèrôme's famous marble *Omphale*, the Lydian queen who enslaved and later married Hercules. What does it mean, to protect a representation of oneself while remaining exposed? The fact that Dupont is covering the artwork while Gérôme cleans up points to a collaborative relationship between the artist and his muse. On the stand lies a tiny vermillion flower, an offering, like the showers of roses tossed by adoring audience members at the end of a spectacular performance. There is a sweetness to the scene, a simple intimacy between the artist and the model that makes me think that maybe Pygmalion and Galatea *did* live happily ever after, after all.

The first time I modeled for a group of sculptors, I thought *this must be what it feels like to be a planet.* The modeling stand stood in the middle of the studio, rather than against one wall. The walls were white, the stand was white and I though the floor was white too until I realized it was covered with a thin layer of fine white porcelain dust. The casters of their sculpting stands left tracks in it as the sculptors orbited me like dervishes. I was used to the sensation of eyes upon me, but I was completely unused to feeling those eyes move around me, of having them move through my line of sight like constellations across the night sky and then disappear as if under a horizon. I was grateful to be sitting down, my bare butt firmly planted on the sheet-covered stool, because I felt like I might float off into space. At the end of the session the floor itself was art: the tracks made by the paths of the sculptors working in the round had blurred together into a single circle: the *ensō* of Zen calligraphy, created in one meditative brushstroke—representing everything and nothing.

Posing is a form of meditation. I find a focal point somewhere in the middle distance: a light switch, a dent in the wall, an object on a shelf that I know won't be moved. As I relax, I can feel my field of vision grow astonishingly wide. As I grow uncomfortable, an inevitability no matter how comfy the pose seems at first, my field of vision shrinks back to that focal point. If the pose becomes excruciating, as they often do, nothing but that focal point exists—a vignette in a silent film slowly fading to black—and I count to ten over and over until the timer goes off. Then I rub feeling back into limbs, sip some water, and stretch as much I can in the five-minute break before heading back to the stand for another twenty minutes of complete immobility. Repeat for three hours, sometimes four.

I pride myself on rarely breaking a pose, on creating interesting shapes with my body that won't leave me with nerve damage although I typically lose circulation in some body part or another. I may not be the most agile or athletic figure model you could hire, but I can stay very, *very* still.

What did Emma Dupont think about as she fixed her gaze on some dent in Gérôme's studio wall? Was she thinking about how the pins and needles in her right foot had long subsided into numbness? Was she wondering what happened to the boy she accompanied to Paris so many years before, the one she thought was her destiny but who abandoned her once they reached the big city? Did she take the pain she felt in her strained back, her numb toes, her grumbling stomach and send it all out in a wordless curse upon him, wherever the hell he may be?

It's a lot harder to pose for a portrait than for a figure drawing. While sitting for a portrait, you have to remain aware of what your face is doing, of how emotions will inevitably pass over it like clouds over a summer field. Skilled portrait artists can capture a moment's expression, arrest a fleeting emotion rather than create a composite of the model's face over the course of several hours. It helps them achieve this if you can empty your mind.

Artists invariably comment on my stillness and ask me how I do it. If I feel like they can take my dark sense of humor, I tell them the truth—that I've been forced to dissociate in order to survive so much of my life that I've honed it into a superpower. I feel a kinship with Fernande Olivier, who fled an abusive marriage in 1900, renamed herself, and started modeling for Picasso. In her memoir—which she used to extort enough money out of Picasso to support herself after he dumped her for another model—she describes her own experience of dissociation while posing:

> *To pose well you have to forget you're posing... forget life, forget who you are, lose yourself in another life completely within yourself, a life that's filled with a happiness you could never find except in our dreams. Luckily I have this facility for dividing myself in two, which is ideal for this exhausting job.*

Picasso painted over sixty portraits of Olivier, but my favorite is *Fernande with a Black Mantilla*. In Picasso's painting, the same sad poet eyes of the girl in the red leather armchair gaze at you out of a French face. The fog of the gray background drips and splatters onto her shoulders like bird droppings. She looks like a woman who has been through things that taught her how to divide herself in two.

Gazing at Olivier's tired-beyond-caring expression I remember weeping in front of Käthe Kollwitz's 1904 self-portrait, one of the fifty or so she made in her lifetime, in which she looks so exhausted by all the horrors she's seen that I wanted to hold her. The Kollwitz Museum in Köln is tucked into the top floor of an office building, and I had a hell of a time finding it. I was determined, however, to make a pilgrimage to see one of the artists I admired so much when I was young. She inspired me to draw self-portraits. I tried to make them as honest as possible, like hers, which was probably another thing prompted my teacher's concern. Wiping my eyes, I found a poster of the drawing and carried it in my arms all the way back home, where I tacked it up on the wall. My husband hated it.

"I just don't get why you would want to look at something so depressing every day. Didn't you say it made you cry?"

What I couldn't explain to him, the man who left bruises on my arms and holes in our walls, was that that through all the horror that went on behind those closed doors, Käthe Kollwitz was my only witness. That her gaze held mine and said *I see you*.

Jean-Léon Gérôme was not the only French sculptor who saw himself in Pygmalion. Auguste Rodin, a veritable titan of sculpture, carved his name next to the mythical sculptor's on his rendition of *Pygmalion and Galatea*. This Pygmalion is an undeniable self-portrait. Bearded and past his prime, his face is nearly buried in Galatea's belly. Her gaze is averted, and she leans away, her legs locked in rough marble up to the knee as she leans on an a very phallic protuberance of stone. In Rodin's sculpture it is impossible to tell in what state of metamorphosis she is: statue or woman. Is she trapped somewhere in between? Is this Pygmalion-Rodin an assailant or a madman trying to seduce a chunk of marble? Does it matter? What matters is this: he looks like Hemingway by way of Jerry Garcia, which is to say he looks like my father. He looks like that one painter whose phone calls I never answer after five in the evening because I know he'll be drunk and because if he ever got creepy with me it would break my heart.

I count myself incredibly lucky that I've never had any inappropriate encounters during my art modeling career. Even that one painter—a real Old World-style master with a dirty old man reputation—has been nothing but respectful to me. "You're the only model I've ever seen him *not* paint bigger breasts on," one of his colleagues commented. The tiny oil he produced from the hundred hours I spent in one pose still hangs on his wall with an astronomical price tag under it. By the time I finally found the courage to leave my marriage, terror had whittled my body down to ninety pounds and modeling was the only place I knew peace. His studio was my sanctuary.

I felt like the luckiest person alive every morning I climbed the stairs to his studio and stepped back in time: Shelves of old books, plaster busts. Brushes and jars of hand-ground pigments. The smell of rabbit-hide glue drying on foolscap, linseed oil and turpentine, fresh coffee and brindled dog. Morning light from the high windows bathed it all in rosy gold, and every twenty minutes I would get up and stretch before padding around in his bathrobe, sipping coffee and trying hard to burn it all into my memory forever.

This is also why I do it: to stop time. To suspend a moment like a pearl on a string. Or like that one perfect cabochon opal once tipped into my palm as payment.

In 2011, a previously unknown painting of Emma Dupont came up for auction in Paris. The pose, used as a reference for Gèrôme's *Pool in a Harem*, looks like it would've been hell to hold for long. Dupont is lying propped on her elbows and left hip, twisted around to face the viewer so that her buttocks and breasts are on full display. She gazes out directly at you with a knowing little smile. This isn't the expression of a model white-knuckling her way through pain by dissociating. She's *flirting* with you. It's a shockingly contemporary piece depicting a woman in full possession of herself, and here's the best part: *the painting belonged to her.* Emma Dupont's descendants put it up for auction that December, and while I could never imagine parting with such a treasure, I can imagine it hanging in Emma's little Parisian apartment. I can see a silver-haired Emma pausing to stand before it as she sips her morning café au lait, smiling at her younger self from across the span of a life well-lived. ■

Works Referenced

Olivier, Fernande. *Loving Picasso: The Private Journal of Fernande Olivier.* New York: Abrams, 2001.

Waller, Susan. "Jean-Léon Gérôme's Nude: Emma Dupont: The Pose as Praxis". *Nineteenth-Century Art Worldwide: A Journal of Nineteenth-Century Visual Culture*, Vol. 13, Issue 1, 2014. http://www.19thc-artworldwide.org/spring14/new-discoveries-jean-leon-gerome-s-nude-emma-dupont . Accessed 18 March 2023.

NIGHTJARS

Doomed to wander, nightjars
have a habit of resting

and roosting on roads. Gathering
strength to sing, they might also

be rewriting melodies. As a boy,
in the dark, I made myself

as flat as I could be under
the covers. On the top bunk,

I used to sing myself to sleep.
Here Comes the Rain Again, but

hymns, mostly: *Make Me
a Channel of Your Peace, How

Great Thou Art.* I sang loudly.
Too loudly, it seemed—my parents

came separately, knocking
politely on my door, asking me

to *rejoice a little more quietly.*
I remember my mother said

exactly that. *Moonlighting*
or *Dallas* was on. But those

songs filled me up and moved
me like wind: *Then sings my soul!*

and *Oh, Master, grant that I may
never seek.* Those are not quiet

words! But I sang softer, just
to myself, so my voice would

never leave the room. *National
Geographic* maps were pinned

to my walls. My loneliness
roamed around the continents, across

disputed borders, plumbed the sea
for notable rifts and trenches.

I thought everyone
felt all the feelings.

JOHN BROOKS

MET

In an orca-colored room,
we glare into a jungle

which is actually Paris.
I tell you I loved Rousseau

when I was a young man;
I am a young man and love

Rousseau, you say. His half-coy
beast, concerned with repast

and eyeing something delicious
on Bonnard's adjacent terrace,

pays us no mind. It's morning—
there's so much time—the king

is feeding, perhaps on a crocodile.
We skip Vincent's wind-whirled

cypresses, Renoir's hideous carmine
cheeks, and pass through ancient

lands: Phoenicia, with her serene
sarcophagi, and Babylon, where

a small, smooth frog was used
to measure weight. *I want to*

carve stone, you say. Feldspar,
hematite, if you can find it.

There's only so much time.
We are leaping through gold

dust brume, backward into what
is now someone else's shame.

Islands, romance, banquets
lie ahead, if we're lucky...and

if we're not, there is rose water
and war. But we are happy, kiss

anyway, step out into lamplight,
into city light, into a shower

of glowing meteors, and I am
at your feet, judging love's

riddling timbre. You carry a trio
of hot soups; the miso blooms

in the broth. After days of rain,
the garden is open again; I turn

around to look at the flowers
and two women are grinning

at us. Their little dog lives
in a house for nothing. Under

your Wranglers, your underwear
is light blue and a little shiny,

like abalone, and barely
holds it all in.

JOHN BROOKS

LAKEHOUSE II

Lake silence, no night
song, no dawn chorus,

the birds already flown
south, the frogs burrowed

in the benthos. It's autumn,
but almost warm. Young enough

to brave the chill, we debate
one last swim. I'm picking apples

with my eyes, scanning the ledge
across the water for delicious reds

amidst the ochres, titians, sepias.
This is a real backwoods town;

we download Grindr to see
what it's like, but already know

each tiger, each somatic
archetype. Conner says

there's a ninety-nine year old
owl spirit just a few towns

over, but he's an expensive
kind of lady. I text my man

a picture of me in bed and
he replies *could you try to be*

a little less beautiful? A blue
sheet covers my lower body

like I'm half-submerged.
David has been writing

haikus; in an antique shop,
he bought an old copper

teapot. I considered
a pair of porcelain

geese, one of which
was marked *damaged,*

but when I looked,
I couldn't find

the flaw.

JOHN BROOKS

WORTH
SAVING

MINDY MISENER

Now that he was fifty-eight, Harvey could say that success was not a matter of vision or inspiration. Even hard work wouldn't suffice. Success happened when you did what made sense. When you didn't try to see too far into the future. Success involved a certain faith—that things would work out, particularly if you didn't think too much about them. This faith was his strength.

Other strengths: in the shop he was finicky about things getting put away (nothing got lost, the place was relatively clean), he spoke rapidly but not at length (people listened), he conferred with customers right there in the wide garage entrance, half in the sunny world of traffic and trees and half in the cool shade of the shop (he knew where to situate people so they were at ease). He did good work. He hired good men. Raymond Auto had a good reputation, and a ditty on the radio.

But at home Harvey lived in corners—the basement, where he had a workbench covered with small appliances he was planning to fix; his small study with the big metal desk; the garage; the yard; the far end of the dining room table. The house was Marion's stage, and it was her scarves draped over the backs of chairs, her rings left on a table, and her paperbacks with the pretty covers that seemed the important props. They'd met on a cold spring night in 1971, when she marched over to where he was sitting and told him he was the only person in the room she didn't know and he had better tell her who he was quick because she hated being out of the loop. He'd wanted to stand but couldn't because of the way she leaned over him, her features looming like a painting about to fall off a wall.

Harvey didn't mind that Marion outshone him. There are times a man wants to fill a room and there are times he doesn't. He wanted to live simply. He wondered sometimes if his career and his standing were preventing him from living in service to a kind of thinking. Or not a kind of thinking but a kind of waiting. Harvey had long had the feeling that if everything could just hold still long enough, he would know what would become of him, or what had already become of him. Maybe, he thought, this private waiting-for-reckoning is

just something that happens as a person got older. He waits
for judgment. He waits for a decision. He waits for a word, a
sign. He does not know what he waits for. And as he waits,
in those semi-private corners of the house he's shared with
his wife of almost forty years, he lets the banister get wobbly
and the water stain on the bedroom ceiling grow like a lake
in rain. He doesn't bother to take clippers to the tall grasses
around the base of the house when he mows the lawn, which
is infrequently. And the night before his wife's gallbladder
surgery, he forgets, on his way home from work, to pick up the
takeout she's ordered.

■ ■ ■

"Remember?" Marion asked, holding the phone to her ear
while she waited for the Italian place to pick up, so she could
change their order to delivery. "I told you I refuse to cook my
own Last Supper." She was a strange mixture of fatalistic and
unfazed: she seemed to enjoy the prospect of going under as
much as she did the prospect of waking up changed. She'd
bought herself a new blouse to wear to the hospital. She'd
ordered potted plants for the living room because she'd read
that plants speed the healing process. Harvey thought she
was going overboard. The surgery, after all, was optional. But
Marion said, "I have a life to live!" Like every happy event was
waiting on the other side of the O.R.

"I'm sorry," said Harvey, offering as an excuse the delayed
delivery of a radiator hose, the unhappy customer. Actually,
Troy had been the one who'd called the customer to say they
were a day behind, but the setback still weighed on Harvey. He
didn't like letting anyone down—including, of course, Marion,
who interrupted him with a raised finger when someone at the

Italian place picked up. After she hung up, she stared at the wall for a long moment, then said, simply, "It's okay. I know you're busy." Her offhanded tone made Harvey's heart ache a little.

In the morning Harvey drove his wife to the same university hospital they'd gone to for years. When they were in their twenties she had delivered two babies there. One of them made it a few hours, the other was gone before it came out. There were a couple other false starts, but those didn't involve the hospital, just new sheets and mattress pads.

The hospital was different now. For one, it was much bigger, with new wings and glassy atriums in every direction, so that Harvey couldn't even make out the original L-shape of the building. Another difference was now they had something called Teams. Marion's Team had a senior doctor named Radcliffe, a nurse, a resident, and two interns. The nurse looked like she smoked. (Harvey had quit years ago but he was still good at guessing about other people.) For some reason this impression pleased Harvey.

"Everyone here?" Dr. Radcliffe asked. "Everyone ready?"

"Ready as any old bag of bones could be," said Marion. The Team's attention had made her girlish, and she was practically batting her eyes at Dr. Radcliffe, who must've been at least fifteen years younger than she was. He looked both lanky and taut, the sort of person who probably ran marathons for fun.

Marion said, "If you all are the Team, what does that make me? The ball? The water girl?"

"The captain," said one of the interns. He was blonde, big-boned, pink-cheeked. It seemed he didn't move unnecessarily, or at least not without thinking about it first. In this way he reminded Harvey of a cow.

"Well," said Marion, too flustered to reply before Harvey gave her one last peck on the cheek and they wheeled her away.

■ ■ ■

One spring, back when Harvey and Marion were still counting on children, Troy came in with the news that Priscilla Leavensworth had lost control of her car over on the hills on the west side of town. She'd driven into an apple orchard. Her back was hurt—there was the possibility of paralysis. Troy didn't have to say her car had been in the shop the week before. Harvey remembered. He knew her as a stingy divorcee with a dumpy old car she drove erratically. She'd come in complaining about grinding brakes. After Troy had finished with the linings he called Harvey to look at the tie rods. Troy was right, the connection was weak. Harvey knew she'd accuse him of inventing problems in order to earn a buck, but he told Troy he'd talk to her about it. Later, though, when she came in and stood too close to his desk while he drew up the bill, he didn't bring it up. He could have come up with a reason to explain himself: he wanted to go home. He was tired. She was a pain. She wouldn't pay for it anyway. Plenty of cars have imperfect steering systems. As he remembered it, though, he hadn't had a *reason* to not bring it up. Bringing it up was just something he didn't do.

"If Priscilla drives off a cliff," Harvey told Troy, "that's not our problem."

Troy moved his jaw to one side and back again.

"We did our job," said Harvey. "You know we did."

Troy was still a new hire, and all Harvey really knew about him was that he'd been born in the same year as Harvey, that his wife Patty was a shy, thick-thighed redhead, and that Troy and Patty were Christians. Troy kept a Bible at the shop, which he read while he ate lunch. Harvey had not yet decided how he felt about this.

After telling Troy to get back to work, Harvey worked out his testimony—he'd repeat, calmly, that he *had* told Priscilla there looked like a potential problem with the steering system. Priscilla would grow more and more upset. Harvey would at one point turn to her and remind her that maybe she had been too upset about the bill to register his warning. He'd be reprimanded for speaking directly to her, and would be contrite, but the judge would grant him a brief, knowing look—*some women just don't listen.*

So Harvey, sometimes heartened and sometimes dismayed by his defense, waited for the fallout. But no word of an investigation, or even of an accusation, ever reached him.

So Harvey, sometimes heartened and sometimes dismayed by his defense, waited for the fallout. But no word of an investigation, or even of an accusation, ever reached him. Either the accident was Priscilla's fault, and she knew it, or it wasn't actually her fault, but she knew enough about her driving abilities and her cheap junky car to blame herself anyway.

By the time it became clear the Priscilla business would not come back to them, Harvey and Troy had changed the way they worked. They spent longer than necessary explaining things to their customers—customers who were, increasingly, women who'd heard about how attentive, even sensitive, they could be. They didn't invent or hype potential problems. *Now this would be mighty unlikely, but...* Their tones were gentle. *The extra cost is, of course, something to consider.*

Business was good.

Harvey did not anticipate that, a year later, Troy would come into Harvey's office and use the word "breakdown" (it would take Harvey a minute to realize he wasn't talking about a car). Troy would talk vaguely but at length about guilt. He would talk about lying by omission. Harvey would have to find a way to calm him down. Doing so would take time and effort and a series of after-work conversations, but Troy would stay on. He'd be Harvey's most loyal employee.

■ ■ ■

Two hours didn't seem like a long time until Harvey skimmed an entire *Time* magazine, cover to cover, in six minutes. He wandered to the cafeteria, getting lost twice in the process despite stopping to look at every color-coded map he saw.

The cafeteria had a whole curved wall of windows looking west. He was looking out those windows when the woman in line in front of him whirled around to ask him what he wanted. She didn't have cash, she explained, and her order didn't meet the five-dollar credit card minimum. Harvey told her, and was then embarrassed for not offering to pay for *her* food. He tried to pay her back, but she resisted. They took their food to a table by the windows. Her name was Anne, and her sister was having a lumpectomy. Harvey said his wife was having her gallbladder out. They commented on the big windows and the view. Anne pointed toward where she lived. Harvey pointed toward where he worked (his house was in a direction they couldn't see). "I work at an auto body shop," he said. "It's that way."

He liked introducing his work in this order: he was a mechanic. Where? Over at Raymond Auto—the one down on

River Road. Well, yes, he was Harvey Raymond. He was glad to hear their reputation was so good—thanks for saying so.

"You dress well," Anne said. The juice she'd ordered was green. She managed to smile back at him even as she drank from the bottle.

Harvey had cheated twice. The first was a hurried, three-time thing that both of them lost interest in. The second lasted a couple months, until the woman started talking about Harvey leaving Marion (the woman said "your wife"). It was the way the woman thought she could plan Marion's future that bothered Harvey. He broke off the affair, barely slept for a week, told Marion. It was terrible, that whole long process—coming clean, summoning the details Marion demanded, asking again and again for forgiveness. He did not tell her about the first affair: the second confession seemed to cover the first offense. Since then he'd had maybe two other opportunities, but they'd been customers who didn't pay attention when Harvey tried to explain the diagnostics he'd done on the ignition coils or how a neglected spark plug could mean a whole new catalytic converter. And Harvey didn't like people who couldn't listen.

Harvey asked what Anne did.

"I have a TV show. It's called *Take Two*."

"It sounds familiar," he said.

"Don't lie."

"It does," he insisted, because it did. "It's a show that covers—it's about—" He laughed.

"A features show," she said. "Local interest." She drained the rest of her juice, put her hands on the creases of her hips, looked at the landscape behind Harvey's shoulder.

"It sounds interesting."

"It is," she said, "sometimes." Then she said, "My sister is driving me nuts. She's being a drama queen about this whole thing."

"Me, too. I mean with my wife."

"It's like she's having brain surgery or something, but they don't even know if the lump is cancerous or not. When some of us know what cancer is like. Some of us have worn wigs. Some of us have had mastectomies."

Harvey's eyes went to her blouse. She laughed. He blushed.

"So tell me about your wife," she said. "How's she being a drama queen?" She was sitting up straighter now, her expression intent and measured.

"Oh," he said, thinking Anne's sister sounded worse than Marion. "Everything's a bit overblown with Marion. She likes excitement."

"Likes excitement how?"

"I just think she gets bored sometimes."

"What does she do?"

"She doesn't work. But she volunteers, and has her clubs, and dates with friends."

"So she keeps busy."

"She likes being busy."

"And do you see the surgery as just another way for her to stay busy?"

"I don't know," he said, wanting the questions to stop

Anne sat back a little. "Sorry. I get into work-mode."

"It's okay."

"It's a little rude. But anyway." She pinched the tiny face of her watch between her thumb and forefinger. "I'd better go. Wish me luck."

"Good luck," he said, and watched her as she neatly dropped the empty juice bottle into a recycling bin. Then she slid her hands into the pockets of her slacks and walked away, elbows bobbing.

■ ■ ■

Harvey wandered the hospital halls, trying to get lost, failing to. He wanted to run into Anne. He wanted to get a little farther with her line of questioning. But he didn't see Anne and the halls made him feel like he was underground, so he left the hospital and drove over to the shop, where Troy was taking an early lunch with Patty. The two of them sat at a dilapidated picnic table behind the shop. Harvey couldn't remember the last time he'd seen her. Her hair had dulled, like she'd spent the last few years in an attic. She pulled Tupperware out of a sack and stacked them neatly in front of Troy, like they were her wares.

Harvey sat in his office and frowned at some paperwork until it was time to go. He stopped for flowers on the way back. Big orange lilies in yellow paper.

As soon as he walked into the waiting room the receptionist said, "Harvey Raymond?" and Harvey said yes and she said, "Wait right there." She made a call. Within a minute Dr. Radcliffe was on the other side of the room, motioning Harvey over.

"We've been calling you," he said.

"I stepped out," said Harvey, hoisting the flowers a bit.

"There's been a complication with the surgery," Dr. Radcliffe went on. "We touched an artery."

The surgeon wasn't looking at him. For a whole long moment Harvey tried to make sense of this man who had killed his wife. Marion.

"She's no longer in critical condition," Dr. Radcliffe said. "She's unconscious, but you can see her."

Too dazed for relief, Harvey followed him to the room where they'd brought her. Maybe it was the size of the bed or the fact that it looked like a crib or the blood she'd lost—and how much blood *had* she lost, the thought made him sick— but she looked half her normal size. At night when she slept her lips twitched and she smiled, but now her face was still. Harvey took stock of the tubes connecting her to the machines and picked up her light, limp hand.

The nurse from the Team came in, then. She looked at what the machines said and took some notes. She touched Marion's foot.

"Why'd you do that?" Harvey asked.

"I like to let them know I'm here," she said, without looking at him.

"Were you there? What happened?"

"I was there all right," she said. By now the faint smell of her recent cigarette had reached him. "Paul didn't know that a cauterizing knife works both ways. Apparently he's only

At night when she slept her lips twitched and she smiled, but now her face was still. Harvey took stock of the tubes connecting her to the machines and picked up her light, limp hand.

used traditional knives. But you just *touch* an artery with the cauterizing knife, and…Your wife's a lucky woman." She slid the pen into a holster at the top of her clipboard.

"Which one is Paul?"

"The intern. Big guy." She put her hands out to show him. "*I* coulda told him about that knife. Jesus Christ."

"I wish you had," said Harvey.

"I do too," she said. "But it's not in my job description, telling people things they're supposed to know."

"Of course," said Harvey. "It's just, I'm a little shaken up."

"You and Paul both. He disappeared into a laundry room somewhere." Then she said, "You should go home. Don't do anything heroic like spend the night here. Save that for when she's *actually* dying."

Harvey hesitated.

"What do you want me to say? 'I'm not going to let her die'? Because I won't."

"Okay," said Harvey, and gathered his coat.

"Good boy," she said. "My guess is she'll be up around lunchtime."

■ ■ ■

But Marion was awake by nine in the morning, which was when Harvey returned. They'd moved her to a room with flowered wallpaper and fewer machines. She was sitting up, her hair brushed, the blankets smooth. Without makeup on she looked both older and more innocent than usual. A different nurse was adjusting her blankets.

"Did they tell you I almost *died*?" she asked, beaming.

"I'm so glad you didn't," said Harvey, bending awkwardly to hug her.

"I don't remember a *thing* except that I woke up a few hours ago and everyone applauded. Imagine if every morning each of us woke up to applause: 'You're here! You're alive! Praise be!'"

The nurse chuckled.

"All I'm saying," Marion went on, "is tomorrow morning I'm going to wake up and I can guarantee there'll be no applause. All Harvey here is going to say is, 'Will you scratch my back?'"

"That's husbands for you," said the nurse.

Harvey wished Marion hadn't mentioned it. Mornings were when he felt vulnerable, uncertain, not himself. And he didn't ask for a back scratch *every* morning. In fact he tried not to ask more than once or twice a week. Marion typically complied for a few minutes, and his gratefulness when she did brought on the sort of ache that comes before crying. Her fingernails, filed to soft points and drawing a slow scribble on his back, somehow brought him back to himself, to his room, to the comfort of not just knowing where and who he was but of feeling those things, facts instead of mirages.

They gave her five big balloons on her way out. The balloons made tapping noises when they bumped together and totally obstructed Harvey's view out the back of the car. Two blocks from the hospital, he almost got in an accident changing lanes. Marion slapped her knees and laughed.

"I'm a charm," she said.

At home the first thing she did was tie the balloons to the curved back of the rocking chair. The second thing she did was sit in Harvey's office for three hours, calling all of her friends to tell them how she almost died. At dinner she listed everyone she'd talked to, as well as their reactions: some cried in relief, others were outraged, a few chided her for going to the university hospital in the first place.

"I guess we've always gone there before," Harvey said. "And it's so close."

"Not only that," said Marion, "but like I've always said, I'm proud to be a part of those young doctors' educations."

Of course Harvey could not remember a single time Marion had ever said this.

"And I said so, to Patty and Yuma and Clark. What they *really* couldn't believe is what I want to do about it." She let a long silence hang.

"What do you want to do about it?"

"I'm going to have Paul do the surgery again."

"Marion."

"I already asked him this morning. Before you arrived. He came by to see me. Did you know he spent two hours sobbing in a linen closet yesterday?"

"Because *he almost killed you.*"

"He told me he stayed up half the night writing a letter to all his family and former teachers explaining that he didn't have what it took."

"I'm surprised he slept at all."

"You know what else he said? That giving him this chance is the greatest thing anyone's ever done for him." She gave him a fierce look. What was Harvey supposed to do? Say, "Go ahead, I think it's a great idea"? Harvey did not think it was a great idea. He didn't think Marion would die at the hands of the young intern. What bothered him was how she was trying to be the hero in this kid's life. What bothered him was she'd probably pull it off.

■ ■ ■

Harvey and Troy were mostly in the habit of leaving their private lives at home, but the day he went back to work Harvey couldn't help but explain that not only had Marion almost died at the hands of a dimwit intern but now she wanted the intern to have another chance at the surgery.

"Sheesh," said Troy, which was as close as he ever came to a curse. "You tried to talk her out of it?"

"I've done everything but flat out forbid it," Harvey said. He liked the way it sounded like flat-out forbidding it would work.

"You don't want to resort to that," Troy said. Harvey couldn't tell whether or not Troy was speaking from experience. What might Troy have to forbid Patty from? Harvey hadn't the foggiest. When he first hired Troy, he'd thought they'd end up buddies, gingerly helping each other through the tough stuff, supportive but not too hands-on. But after Priscilla's accident Troy had needed so much. In a way Harvey had appreciated how hard Troy had seemed to be listening to him. But Harvey had not enjoyed playing the counselor. Sure, Troy eventually moved on, and sure, maybe Harvey had a hand in that, but he also knew that in the end you couldn't change a man's mind.

"Let me know if you want to talk," said Troy, looking at the wrench he was turning over in his hands.

"Want to grab lunch?" Harvey said. It wasn't that he wanted Troy's advice—what he wanted was that shared agreement. "We can go down to Miss Curtis." The Miss Curtis Diner served the best powdered donuts for a hundred miles.

Troy pointed the wrench toward the Impala in front of him. "I'll just finish this first."

Harvey went to his office to wait for lunchtime. *I like Troy*, Marion used to say. *Despite his politics*, she'd add. She'd ask why Harvey didn't spend more time with him and Harvey would give her vague answers. She didn't know about the Priscilla business, though once she'd referred to that cranky woman in a wheelchair. Eventually she gave up on Troy, just like she gave up on all the other male friends she'd tried to press on Harvey.

He looked toward the clock and saw Anne on the other side of the door to his office. He waved her in.

"I found you," she said.

"So you did."

She settled into the wood chair across from Harvey without his even inviting her to. She arranged her leather purse on her lap and crossed her legs. "Did you know you have very good reviews online?" she asked. She needed his advice: she'd overheard people in line at the grocery store talking about how a friend of theirs was going to need a whole new very expensive something-or-other because he hadn't replaced this certain belt.

"The timing belt?" Harvey asked.

"That's it. The timing belt."

Harvey asked about the make of her car and how many miles it had. He explained that 65,000 miles was on the low side for a new timing belt.

"It depends on what kind of person you are," he said. "You could give it another ten or twenty thousand miles if you wanted. It's not a safety thing, just a big expense if the belt goes and you need a new longblock."

Harvey explained the variables—driving style, the tiny but important differences between cars, even of the same model, weather, type of driving. "But even if you told me all those things, I couldn't say for sure."

"You're not going to advise me one way or another?"

"I'm going to give you the information you need to make the decision yourself."

"I like that about you."

"I like that you listen." A moment of frank intimacy ensued. Harvey held Anne's eyes, then dropped his own.

"Do you want to get lunch?" she asked.

Harvey looked through the wall of windows into the garage. Troy was wiping his hands on a cloth and frowning at an intake valve. "I have plans," he said.

"No problem." She seemed about to stand. "Thanks for the advice."

Harvey said, "How's your sister?"

"Acting like she's back from the brink of death, of course. How's your wife?"

"Back from the brink of death," said Harvey.

Anne laughed, then saw his expression. "You're serious?"

As Harvey explained what had happened her face became grave and displeased. She said she was so sorry; she said it was terrible; she said she couldn't imagine. Harvey told her about Marion wanting Paul to do the surgery again.

"Oh my," Anne said. "I can't say that's the decision I'd make." She paused. "Then again, it's also quite generous of her."

"It is," said Harvey.

"This would be perfect for the show, you know."

"I hadn't thought of that," he said, truthfully.

"It's my job to think of these things. Give it a little thought. Ask your wife." She pulled a business card from her purse, set it on the glass top of Harvey's desk. "In the meantime, my best to Marion."

"Thank you. And let me know what you decide about the timing belt. I mean, if you decide to have the work done here."

"If anywhere, it will be here," she said, and left.

It wasn't unusual for Harvey to have a woman in his office, but while he and Troy waited for their food at Miss Curtis, Harvey found himself explaining that Anne had come in for a consultation and it turned out she not only had a TV show but wanted to do a segment on Marion.

"Patty watches that show," said Troy, when Harvey told him which one.

"Marion probably watches it too," said Harvey, though actually he had no idea. He hadn't told Troy about meeting Anne at the hospital, and he knew he wouldn't.

"Are you asking for my opinion?" Troy said.

"Yeah," said Harvey, realizing he was—even though Troy didn't know the whole situation, or maybe because Troy didn't know the whole situation. In any case, he wanted to let himself be influenced.

"I think a lot of good could come from it. And I think it would be fun for Marion."

"Those are both true," said Harvey.

"You seem a little down about it."

"A lot's been happening."

"I know," said Troy, twirling his straw wrapper. "For what it's worth, I'm praying for you."

"Thanks."

"Okay, I'm putting God stuff away now."

"You don't have to," said Harvey, but was glad he did.

■ ■ ■

At first Harvey didn't bring up *Take Two* with Marion because he didn't trust his own motives. But then he started thinking about how much this experience meant to Marion, and how she would want to share it with other people. He let this second line of reasoning overtake the first. He told Marion and was at first surprised by her reluctance.

"I thought you'd love it," he said. "You've seen the show, right?"

"I've seen it. But I don't know." She was bashful, unsure. "I hate being on camera," she added.

Well, this was true. As soon as any camera appeared Marion began a nervous frenzy of primping and smoothing. In photographs she looked stiff, slightly unhappy.

"You're going to be unconscious for the action."

Marion gave a little huff that wasn't quite a laugh. "I thought you didn't want me to do this."

"I didn't," he said. "But you're doing a good thing."

"What about Paul? What if he doesn't want to be on the show?"

"Then of course we won't do it. I thought it would be fun for you," he said. "That's why I mention it. We could have a little viewing party here—wouldn't that be nice?" Marion was always asking to have a party at the house and Harvey was always resisting.

She thought a moment. "I know I'm being a ninny. Right after the surgery I was so confident about everything. It's like it finally hit me—I almost died. I could be dead right now." She started to cry. Harvey sat close to her, smoothed the sleeve of her sweater.

"You don't have to have surgery," he said. "Or you can go somewhere else. We can go to the nicest hospital in Boston."

"You're sweet," she said. They sat together for a while, saying nothing, until the phone rang. She took the phone into the kitchen. It was some friend of Marion's, of course, and Marion's voice mixed with the tap and clatter of emptying the

There was no real way to pick apart the boundaries that separated the things you did and the things that happened to you, no way to say how much nudging something needed before it took on a momentum of its own.

dishwasher. Maybe this Anne thing was over now. The thought made Harvey light, almost happy. Then he heard Marion telling her friend that she'd just been asked to be on a TV show. Marion joking about being a local celebrity. Harvey held still. There was no real way to pick apart the boundaries that separated the things you did and the things that happened to you, no way to say how much nudging something needed before it took on a momentum of its own. No way to know whether anxiety about something happening was because you dreaded that event or wanted it. He thought of Anne's elegant hands, her leather purse. Marion came back into the living room.

"I feel better," she said. "I was just being an old lady."

"I think you're brave," he said, and meant it.

She was looking around the room. "How many people can we fit in here? Twenty? Twenty-five? Or we could have two TVs going—one in here and one in the kitchen. What do you think?"

"Either one could work."

"Oh, Harvey. You *have* to have an opinion," she said.

■ ■ ■

The camera crew was going to come by at the end of the week to start gathering footage—Harvey imagined shots of the house, the yard. But as Harvey played the mental tape, he didn't see an attractive older couple and their modest but handsome house. He saw the water stain on the ceiling and the frayed edge of the living room carpet and the faded brown recliner Marion had been telling Harvey to get rid of for six years now. He took three days off work that week, to address these problems and others. Marion said if she had known that all it took was a little TV show to make Harvey get his act together she would've almost died a whole lot sooner. Marion got her hair cut, dusted the tops of picture frames, filled glass vases with glass pebbles, then drove back to the store for a different color of pebble.

Anne was not with the camera crew when they showed up at the house. Harvey asked where she was, and the short scruffy guy told him that the actual interviews would take place the morning of the surgery, and then of course afterward.

"Harvey," Marion was saying, "we need you over here." He followed her voice into the kitchen. Somehow she had got a dinner going, and Harvey was supposed to sit and make conversation with her while she stirred and chatted. She was fetching in a red sweater and an apron with strawberries on it. Harvey adjusted the way his own shirt tucked into his pants and took his usual seat at the table.

"We can't see you back there," said the scruffy man. "Come on forward. Sit here." He tapped the head of the table, closer to the overhead light.

"He's always sitting back there," Marion said. "Like a kid in a corner."

Harvey sent her a look she didn't receive because she was looking at the insides of a saucepan.

In bed that night he said, "I wish you hadn't called me a kid."

"I said you were *like* a kid," she said. Then she said, "I wonder if I would be doing this if it were someone older who messed up. What if it had been Dr. Radcliffe?"

"He knows how to use the knife."

"He could still screw up," she insisted. "Somehow you want to help a young person. Like there's a point beyond which it's not worth fixing them. But I wonder if I should have let Paul quit."

Harvey was quiet.

"Harvey?" she said.

"I'm thinking," he said. But he wasn't really, just feeling a knot of confusion so tangled he couldn't think.

■ ■ ■

The morning of the surgery, Anne interviewed Harvey and Marion in the living room. Harvey sat next to Marion on the couch and put his arm behind her shoulders and looked at her when she answered questions. When asked for his opinion, he said, "You know, we were talking about this last night—" He paused, and looked at Marion in a way that asked for both permission and forgiveness. He looked back at Anne. "We're childless, you know. But we're thinking, 'What if this were our son? What would we do for him, to give him the confidence he needs? What would we want others to do for him?'"

"Lovely," said Anne.

Marion said, "But you know what? I've thought about it, and I'd give this chance to anybody. Even if they were my age. Even if they were older."

"Why's that?" Anne asked.

"It's like what Harvey said to me last night: the most generous thing we can do for another person is give them a chance to fix their mistakes."

"Not many people can say that," Anne said, her voice a candy apple—smothered in admiration but cool and crisp beneath.

"I said that?" said Harvey, grinning at the camera and then at Anne and then at Marion. Was that what he'd said last night, before falling asleep? "I'm a goddamn poet," he added.

Anne looked at the scruffy man. "We'll cut that," she said.

"Oops," Harvey said, and put his hand on his mouth. But he had meant to say it. He wanted to erase this whole exchange.

■ ■ ■

They rode to the hospital in near-silence. Anne had gone ahead to track down Paul. Marion hummed to herself and watched out the window. She asked Harvey a couple questions about the party—should they do one meat dish, or two? So many people were becoming vegetarians these days, she could never keep them all straight.

Then she said, "I have to tell you something. I invited Troy and Patty."

Harvey waited. "That's all?"

"I wanted you to have a couple friends there. But I should have asked you first."

"It's fine," Harvey said. He imagined Troy looking at him admiringly after the show. He imagined Marion noisily welcoming Patty into the house, showing her around. Why not invite those two in, show them what their lives were about?

"So are they coming?" he asked.

"I left a message," she said.

Harvey decided that if he hadn't heard back from Troy by tomorrow, he'd call him. *Just to invite you myself. Come see the show. Come see the house.* What he would mean was, *Come see what I've made of myself.*

After Marion had been wheeled away—there was a bit of final pre-surgery taping, Harvey holding his wife's hand and kissing her puff of blondish hair—Anne sat next to him. "Want to go down to the cafeteria?"

Harvey looked at her. She was beautiful, and he was not that kind of man anymore. "I don't think so," he said.

She waited for a minute, to see if he'd say anything else, and then she walked away.

■ ■ ■

One week later, twenty people came over for the "little viewing party." Marion's friends took over the whole first floor of the house; they took turns being friendly with Harvey in brief nosy bursts. Troy was late, and came alone; he said Patty wasn't feeling well.

Harvey gave Troy a brief tour of the house, and ended with the basement. He was glad to have an excuse to be away from all that. It had been a long day already.

"I would live down here," Troy said, looking at Harvey's workbench and small rabbit-eared television and cabinet and sink and the stacked appliances Harvey sometimes fixed.

"I practically do," said Harvey.

Troy opened the door of a toaster oven, prodded the disassembled pieces of its heating unit. "Marion miss her toaster?"

"She got a new one. I don't like throwing stuff away if I can fix it."

"This looks about twenty years old," said Troy.

Harvey laughed. "It's been down here for a while."

"Patty and I are getting a divorce," said Troy. His eyes were roving the basement, as if looking for a comfortable place to land.

"I had no idea," said Harvey, honesty making his voice soft. Then he said, "Why?"

"I've been seeing someone else for a while."

"How's Patty taking it?"

"Not good."

"Huh." Harvey wanted to ask a hundred other questions, had they tried counseling, how long had Troy been seeing someone, how long before Patty knew. Wasn't this sort of thing un-Christian? But can a man ever do anything except what makes the most sense? In the end, does a man do anything but take his own counsel?

Harvey sighed heavily, partly because of his own realization and partly because now he couldn't tell Troy the news he had brought him to the basement to tell him: how that very afternoon, while Marion had been puttering in the yard, Paul had called to confess he hadn't done the surgery. He'd assumed he would because he'd agreed to. But when he was scrubbing in Dr. Radcliffe asked him what he thought he was doing. He sent him up to the observation room. Paul hastily tried to describe the situation—Marion's request, the TV show—and Dr. Radcliffe only said he hadn't heard a thing about that and he wasn't going to let Paul near Marion again.

"I was too embarrassed to say anything," said Paul. "I'd already given that TV lady an interview."

"Have you called her? Anne?"

"No," said Paul. "I'm calling her next."

"Do me a favor?" said Harvey. "Don't." Because there was Marion in the back yard, raking the few leaves that had fallen. More would fall, soon. He should be out there, helping her. Harvey said, "If you went around telling everyone, you'd just be asking them to prop you up, to say, *it's okay, you should still be a doctor anyway.* You've got to decide that for yourself." Before he hung up, Harvey said, "That's what I would tell my own son." Then he wondered if he meant it.

■ ■ ■

Marion called down to them. The show was starting.

"I'm sorry," said Troy. "I shouldn't burden you with this."

Harvey nodded, half in agreement, half in acknowledgement that what else was there to do? Some people couldn't make their lives count unless they felt everything had been confessed, accounted for. But silence could be noble, even right.

"Should we go up?" said Harvey, and the two men headed for the stairs, Harvey hoping, ridiculously, that Troy would be heartened by the show. ■

THE LAUNDROMAT POEM

You might / have your very own matching washer-and-dryer set at home /
and never have need for this love song to the lavandería.
–Nikky Finney "From the Washhouse Files"

Every other Sunday starting my junior year, you could find me
folding my fresh clothes at the local laundromat.

Dad's dryer broke and stayed broken and with dad at work
and dirty clothes needing washed we went, just my sister and me

to the nicer spot in the shopping plaza with Shop'n'save and the nail spa.
Notebooks, school books, maybe a boyfriend came with us, some days

nothing—just two teenage girls getting quarters from the wall machine.
I don't know if you've ever been sixteen folding your pink cotton panties

on the plastic countertop along the glass windows
as your catholic school classmates and their mothers moseyed by,

fresh manicures shining, but I wouldn't recommend it, standing there looking
down in your mismatched outfit, lugging loads of laundry in black plastic trash bags,

sitting in silence in the cigarette smoke, even the old ladies
with their stolen shopping carts staring—wondering what the hell you were doing here.

KATE WRIGHT

ARS POETICA AFTER A WISDOM TOOTH EXTRACTION

The doctor told me they had to

                leave it—

the root of my lower right third molar—

    because it was too close

                to my nerve

        too close

                to permanently numb

                lower lip

life of drool

bibs

and never knowing

a harmless thing

the feeling of my lovers

lips,

so they left it

inside,

but my body didn't want it

knew

the thing needed out

so it refused

to heal

hole open in mouth months later

bit by bit

bright white bone

pieces spit

from mouth

to palm

until the day I tired

KATE WRIGHT

dug in

           the relief

and the ripping the ripping the ripping

as out,

      a whole piece of bone.

SESTINA IN WHICH I MISS MY HOMETOWN

"You might / have your very own matching washer-and-dryer set
at home /and never have need for this love song to the lavandería."
–Nikky Finney "From the Washhouse Files"

Every other Sunday starting my junior year, you could find me
folding my fresh clothes at the local laundromat.

Dad's dryer broke and stayed broken and with dad at work
and dirty clothes needing washed we went, just my sister and me

to the nicer spot in the shopping plaza with Shop'n'save and the nail spa.
Notebooks, school books, maybe a boyfriend came with us, some days

nothing—just two teenage girls getting quarters from the wall machine.
I don't know if you've ever been sixteen folding your pink cotton panties

on the plastic countertop along the glass windows
as your catholic school classmates and their mothers moseyed by,

fresh manicures shining, but I wouldn't recommend it, standing there looking
down in your mismatched outfit, lugging loads of laundry in black plastic trash bags,

sitting in silence in the cigarette smoke, even the old ladies
with their stolen shopping carts staring—wondering what the hell you were doing here.

KATE WRIGHT

BACHELOR PANTOUM

It is Monday and the girls are at it again—
sitting, drinking, talking shit. They side eye each other
and take another sip of their pink drinks.
Their crossed-limbed bodies say *No. Don't even try.*

Sitting, drinking, talking shit, they side eye each other,
And I wonder if I could do it—be one of them but
their crossed-limbed bodies *no. Don't even try.*
I read somewhere some girls take out loans to get clothes...

I wonder if I could do it—be one of them but
they are beautiful, even do their own hair and makeup,
I read somewhere. Some girls take out loans. To get clothes—
they have money—maybe only rich girls deserve love

and to be beautiful, even when doing their own hair and makeup,
even in sweatpants. Even when crying. And when they go home,
they have money—maybe only rich girls deserve love
and to be happy but I'm not sure they are happy. Their faces void

even in sweatpants, even when crying, and when they go home.
Every week we watch, hands holding white wine and each others,'
    waiting
to be happy with them, but I'm not sure they are happy.
But it is Monday and the girls are at it again.

KATE WRIGHT

ROSS GAY

J oy and delight. These are two words—two concepts, two states of being, even—that Ross Gay wants his readers to know. In these uncertain times, as our society is increasingly bifurcated and antagonistic, he is insistent that our salvation lies in practicing these two mindsets by walking through the world with an observant reverence and what he calls "caretaking." He describes the latter this way in *The Book of Delights: Essays.* "Holding open doors. Offering elbows at crosswalks. Letting someone else go first. Helping with heavy bags. Reaching what's too high, or what's been dropped. Pulling someone back to their feet. Stopping at the car wreck, at the struck dog." This impulse, Gay believes, "is our default mode and it's always a lie that convinces us to act or believe otherwise. Always."

He is calling on what Lincoln described as "the better angels of our nature." But if you were to mistake this philosophy for some rose-colored, namby-pamby view of the world that makes no room for sorrow or trouble, you would be wrong. All these states, he writes, are all tangled up together. You can't have one without the other.

The author of four poetry collections—including *Be Holding*, which won the PEN American Literary Jean Stein Award, and *Catalog of Unabashed Gratitude*, which received the 2015 National Book Critics Circle Award and the 2016 Kingsley Tufts Poetry Award—Gay published *The Book of Delights*, his debut essay collection, in 2019. The book hit at just the right time. As our world closed in the following year with the onset of the COVID-19 pandemic, the collection found an audience hungry for its compact essays that nudge readers to be on the lookout for wonder in their everyday lives. Gay followed the *New York Times* bestseller with another essay collection, *Inciting Joy*, in 2022. In September, he will release *The Book of (More) Delights*.

Gay spoke with acclaimed poet Ansel Elkins—author of *Blue Yodel*, which received the 2014 Yale Series of Younger Poets prize—about recognizing astonishment, feeling a sense of belonging in and to a place, and his literary influences.

■ ■ ■

Ross Gay

ANSEL ELKINS: The poet Fernando Pessoa wrote that "poetry is astonishment." The act of astonishment seems so central to your poetry, in that many of your poems operate through astonishment, in moments like "To the Fig Tree on 9th and Christian" when something essential is being uncovered like experiencing kindness and shared delight between strangers, or in "Catalog of Unabashed Gratitude," that delivers us to a sudden revelation of "this singing and shuddering" when we realize how brief this life is. When I teach your poems, my students frequently talk about being astonished. Can you talk about the role of astonishment in your writing? How does writing about what astonishes you create the same feeling of astonishment in your reader?

ROSS GAY: Oh, I love that question—because it really gets to one of the things that's so exciting to me about writing, which is how we might be astonished (or perplexed or heartbroken or delighted or, generally, moved) by our own writing. I've lately had the very pleasant experience—more than pleasant actually—of sitting down to write, some sort of journally-type writing, reflecting on what happened the day before or whatever, and feeling excited like I was going to watch a performance by someone whose work I'm very interested in, and who I feel very close to, but have no idea what they're going to do. I can tell you that what comes out, as it comes out, though it is fascinating to me, especially at the time, like so, so fascinating, it would not be to a reader. I mean, it might be fascinating how un-fascinating it is. When I read it a week or two or three later I'm like, hmm. Fascinating how this was so fascinating. And then I revise and yadda yadda etc. All that said! What seems important for me is that feeling of wonder at what I might make, and carrying that wonder through from the beginning to when I decide to be done with whatever it is I'm making. So I guess I'm trying to say that the wonder, the astonishment, is as much in the experience of writing, and the process of writing, as it is in the relationship to the astonishing experience, etc. To figure out how to be astonished throughout the process of conveying astonishment. Something like that.

AE: In "Ode to Sleeping in My Clothes" you connect tree roots with bones and lineage in describing "a man / who has walked to Youngstown, Ohio / from Arkansas without sleeping." You were born in Youngstown (which is technically in Appalachia)—how have your connections with Appalachia influenced your work or identity as a writer?

RG: I truly have no idea. I know I love a lot of writers from or connected to that big ol region. Maurice Manning, Nikky Finney, Shayla Lawson, Gerald Stern, bell hooks, John Edgar Wideman. I don't know if Appalachia claims Toni Morrison; if so, Toni Morrison. But to the extent that Youngstown has influenced my writing (and thinking and being, even though I grew up outside of Philadelphia; Youngstown is where half of my family lived, that is one of our homes), and Youngstown as you say is technically in Appalachia, in addition to that very incomplete list of writers, I'm very, very influenced.

AE: When we met in Berea, where bell hooks taught and where she lived in her final years, we went to the bookstore where you purchased a copy of her book *Belonging*. Your work engages deeply with ideas of beholding, witnessing each other, and belonging to each other. In hooks's

Belonging, there's an essay called "Earthbound on Solid Ground" that made me think of you. In it, she writes, "Before the mass migrations to northern cities in the early nineteen hundreds, more than ninety percent of all Black folks lived in the agrarian South. We were indeed a people of the earth. Working the land was the hope of survival. Even when that land was owned by white oppressors, master and mistress, it was the earth itself that protected exploited Black folks from dehumanization."

In *Inciting Joy* ("Free Fruit for All!") you write about being on a team that established the community orchard in Bloomington, Indiana, which you describe as a free-fruit-for-all food justice and joy project. You write that your product "was the dream of connection" and how the labor of planting that orchard illuminated for you "a matrix of connection, of care, that exists not only in the here and now, but comes to us from the past and extends forward into the future."

Just as I see your work exploring joy as a radical act, how do you connect gardening and your relationship to the natural world as an antidote to "dehumanization"?

RG: Well, I just read a thing about self-driving taxis in San Francisco or whatever. And I think about all the ways people are being made obsolete by this mode of whatever—because it sure as hell isn't a mode of life—in ways we can notice again and again. The objective of this mode it sometimes seems is to just get people out of the way. People being an expense and an encumbrance. (I can hear Wendell Berry in these sentences, and clearly!) Obviously this mode acts much the same with the earth, the land. Oh—the resourceification of everygoddamnthing we might call it. We're all resources, or extractables. And expendables, consequently, too. That seems almost the apex or zenith of this mode of (un)life. And to be in a garden, or an orchard, or on a farm, or in a woods, and deeply so, for me anyway remembers to me what is real, which is not that driverless car making someone filthy rich or a plant genetically modified in a lab to "photosynthesize more efficiently." What is real is the soil, and the seeds, and the trees, and the critters, and the rain, and the sun. Our relationships, and the deepening of them. All this other apparatus that we are so often told is life, and even the good life, is…I was going to say "horseshit" but that would be an insult to horseshit, which is good for the garden.

AE: As a follow up the ways that you write about belonging intersect with the ways bell hooks writes about belonging. Does the sense of place and community of the orchard give you something essential in belonging to this place, these people? I feel that so much of your work is wrestling with how we can belong to each other, how we can create a sense of community, and what is possible when that happens. This seems like a crucial mission during this divisive time in our country's history.

RG: Absolutely. There are all these ways we belong to places, and it seems to me that planting trees with people is a moving one. Loving and tending to the land, and sharing that tending, and that tender, tenderly. I think about that project often, and I often think about how that project helped me to more thoroughly imagine or think about what it means to be a person, you know, in community, in debt, etc. But yeah, to your question, that place, the group of people who came together to make that place (which is still happening, by the way, though I'm no longer involved, aside from going to harvest blackberries every summer and checking on the fig trees that came from my buddy's dad)...there was this dream of something that we entered together, that we kind of made together, and held onto together, sometimes lightly, sometimes firmly, and it seems like the most important part of the dream was what we were doing, which was working on behalf not only of ourselves, but some other people we would likely never meet. In the process, as you can imagine, we became very close—some of those people, who I didn't know before, are now like family.

AE: I see a kinship with Walt Whitman in your work, in your art of digression, in the expansiveness of your spirit, your celebration of the interconnectedness of living beings ("the underground union between us" as you write in *The Book of Delights*) from trees to birds to mulberries to bees—the ode writ large. What does Whitman mean to you as a poet?

RG: Very much, of course, for the catalogs and expansiveness and the spirituality and so much more. But the truth, I think, is that Whitman really comes to me through the poet Gerald Stern, who likewise was a cataloger, a digresser, an expander, deep in the garden, etc. Stern was/is one of my most important poets and mentors and, really, friends. I learned so much from studying his work intensely from the time I was about twenty-two until now. And not only the poems, which are astonishing—I mean, the range he had; the voice—but also the essays, which I think of as among the most beautiful I've read. I go back to all of it frequently, but in the last few years it's been the essays, which my essays are deeply indebted to. *What I Can't Bear Losing, Stealing History, Death Watch.* I think he published the first of those books when he was in his late 70s or early 80s. How grateful we are for him.

AE: What is it like for you as a writer to shift from writing poetry to writing nonfiction? The act of keeping a daily journal could seem far removed from the act of crafting poetry, but in doing this you seem to bring together disparate approaches to writing. Do you feel like you have created a new hybrid form, or do you see your work as an extension of some other genre, such as the *zuihitsu*?

RG: No, no creation of a form—I think of these things as very much in a tradition of folks way back like Montaigne, but coming forward to people like Gerald Stern and others whose work I love like Sarah Manguso and Margo Crawford and Hilton Als, and a zillion others. Oh Brian Blanchfield, etc. God, his essays too. Anyway, yeah, I think I just think of them as little essays. Though, the more I think about it, I might sometimes also relate to them as poems a little bit. Like there are definitely times in these things that I am more guided by the music and the image than the sentence, times that these things think especially musically or something.

AE: Your poems and essays are both wonderfully digressive in form and in how they unfold. Similarly, I notice you use the word "moseying" more than any other contemporary

poet that I know of. "Mosey" is a word I've mostly heard in the rural South, to amble, loaf (as Whitman writes), to walk leisurely or idly, or "hanging out unregulatedly and off the clock" as you write in *Inciting Joy*. Moseying feels almost subversive in our capitalistic society that teaches us to be obsessed with how we "manage" our time and productivity. Can you talk about the importance of digression, or moseying, in your work? Who taught you the art of moseying? What does moseying mean to you?

RG: Oh, here's Gerald Stern again. I think I mean his poems and essays, the way they follow what they need to follow, they take off, and maybe they return to where they seemed to be going, and maybe they don't. You know, I'm not exactly sure how I think about digression in my work, because probably different digressions are different things. Though I do feel like there is something between a reader and writer that is being assumed, or maybe built, when a digression happens. Some kind of trust, because the writer is asking someone to come along, where we don't quite know. Like, *oh, there's this other thing that's calling, do you want to think about that for a few minutes with me? Should we?* I'm interested in that. ■

GENESIS: POET THINKS OF HOME

I was born to a one-story house with ten-story dreams.
Blues grass and dandelions, my mama's wedding bouquet;
cast iron skillets her dowry.
While on duty overnight at the fire station,
my daddy, pistol-packing to work surviving
Sambo jokes and Klan belts strung on city uniforms.

A hungry house still made home:
hot water cornbread, turnip
& mustard greens, butter beans
from my mama's table;
my daddy's ribs and wild game
smoking the grill.
Blessed Sunday dinners,
high ballin' house parties, both
cut on Kentucky bourbon.
Dress to kill and dance to live
'cause they can't stop the music of us.

Beneath the tilted steeple,
Behind the faded stained glass:
usher board schooling, choir rehearsals and
baptist training tainting my girlhood.
Watch ya' mouth! and *Keep your knees together*
in the pew with them thunder thighs.
Pretty is as pretty does
though never telling me
"does who:" or "does what,"
only telling "does not" 'cause

I brought you in this world;
I can take you out though *Jesus*
Loves Me at least at the altar
for the Bible tells me so.

Summer funkshine in every neighborhood:
bottle cap guns, dust bowl tournaments,
the bicycle posse headed for a swim
on the other side of town at the "new pool"
every day 'til my skin freckled, my hair sandied.

Dusk dew droppin' on sticky nights:
"Hide-n-go-seek-go-get it,"
whatever "it" was but
don't get caught with "it," or at "it."
jump rope, jacks, and spades games
as the records played on the porch
with cornrow customers queued, $5 a head.
We taking names and talking game,
me daring myself to not get caught up or
thrown down a rabbit hole
I can't climb out.
have my tail and all the rest of me
in the house before the streetlights blinked
and my mama might think I was contemplating
writing "checks my ass c'aint cash"
—fear of market crash on my family's reputation.

From the pulp of the pulpit to the clout of the projects,
from Oak Grove glory to Mechanicsville,
Bibles bloodied, hammers holy, and families storied.
My soul baptized in Madisonboro. Smell
our blood in the dirt.

TAMARA J. MADISON

CALIFORNIA DREAMING

before she was "Mama"

While others fancied palm trees and beaches,
you envisioned glittery stages,
boas traipsing buttery air
melting beneath the colored lights.
Somewhere there, a place
for all that was you, not just pieces
but all: the fashion, flirtation,
passion waxing jazzy and blue.

Auntie made the trek from Kentucky to Cali,
never looked back except for quick visits on occasion
to see if she had finally made her mama proud.
But your mama, so close, wrapped around your heart,
cried at the thought of your leaving,
cried feeling you out of her reach,
cried until your heart gave and stayed.
Ambition wilted into sin, so you
traveled just across the river, became
the Audrey Hepburn of Madisonboro,
settled for cigarettes between your painted lips,
your hands swirling a highball in fancy glass
cooling the heat of your cheeks,
suitors kneeling at your dancing high-heeled feet.

Little did they know
beneath the high hats and elbow gloves,
under the fox fur stole and strand of pearls,
your heart still lived in faraway places
echoing dreams of L.A.

TAMARA J. MADISON

POSE

Such promise: a strong dark hand covers a fair, dainty one.
Together they hold the knife poised to slice the cake,
guide the blade through the creamy sweetness
only to crumble the fluffy layers.

The arch crowning the cake frames
a miniature plastic bride and groom,
replica of the ideal, they both strive for
as they gaze into the camera, pose,
anchor the knife despite the sweat of their palms.
The groom plants his feet, charms onlookers
with a smile flashing a narrow gap between his teeth.
A tuxedo, classic black, cloaks his muscular frame
always confident on the court but unsure at the altar.
The never bashful bride quietly lowers her eyes,
blushes in a tea-length gown, champagne not white.
The brocade forms a forgiving curtain
covering the softening curves.

Such a flawless affair:
wistful smiles wilting silk,
bittersweet dew on the bouquet and boutonniere,
yet looming beneath these nuptials—
an embryonic blooming,
a budding blemish
(me).

TAMARA J. MADISON

WATCHING GHOSTS

ASHLEY ANDERSON

S ometime during that disorienting week between Christmas and New Year's, my dad twisted himself around in his recliner so he could look at me. "Ashley? Why can't you write stories like that?" As he asked his question, he gestured toward the television where the credits from yet another episode of a black and white western rolled across the screen.

I sat in the corner of the couch, enjoying the beginning of a day visiting my family for the holidays and in which I had nothing planned. I needed a break; the year 2022 had been a whirlwind of many fun and exciting things, but also filled with a lot of writing and work. My dad never remembered what I wrote. He didn't understand why I don't write about him or why I have yet to start on the book he wants me to write about all the years I worked at McDonald's to put myself through school. "Westerns just aren't my thing," I replied.

"Aw, come on! These are good stories!" my dad said, speaking with a mildly incredulous tone. In his world, he couldn't fathom how a person couldn't have the same enthusiasm he did for the fictional adventures of cowboys, U.S. marshals, and pretty women portrayed as vulnerable and in need of protection.

I shrugged my shoulders. Since my dad retired a little over four years ago, I learned that arguing with him about whether or not these were "good stories" was a fool's quest. Logic nor knowledge nor facts gave me leverage because his opinion transcended all those strategies. "Meh. I'm not that kind of writer."

My dad sighed and shifted his weight in the brown recliner where he spent most of his waking and all his sleeping hours. I have grown used to his various forms of dismissal. Simply leaving the conversation was probably the mildest of these forms. I cannot be offended by his behavior, or rather, I have conditioned myself to not be offended. It's not worth the price of adding to my already damaged psyche.

The phrase "good stories" is what wiggles its way under my skin and takes up space. I let my mind wander to a place where my dad's claim of "good stories" insinuates that nothing I could possibly write would be "good." I don't write about cowboys. In fact, I spent many years not writing fiction at all.

While I could puff out my chest and give in to some form of intellectual snobbery, I don't. There is nothing to prove here.

If the precedence holds true, my dad will continue to watch the "good stories" of his beloved westerns. Hour after hour, day after day, the ghosts of these characters will continue their ride across my parents' television screen with my dad held captive in the tales he's watched hundreds, if not thousands, of times before.

■ ■ ■

My dad didn't used to be like this.

He used to be a mixture of goofball and gruff. When I was a small child, pre-school aged, we watched WWE wrestling while rough housing on the living room floor. I would back pedal from the living room to the dining room and run back toward my dad, who laid on his back on the floor. "Flying elbow!" I shouted, plopping on my dad as he laughed at my attempts to imitate what I saw on TV. As my sisters and I grew older, we watched what cartoons we could find on the local channels together. My family didn't have cable television until I was in high school because my parents didn't see the sense in paying for something we already got for free. We became PBS kids because that was the channel where we found shows meant for us.

We watched movies together, even if we found enjoyment in different parts of the films that paraded through the living room. Disney's version of *Tarzan* comes to mind. My dad sat in his recliner by the window and danced along with the soundtrack. My sisters and I attempted to get the combination of "shoos" and "bops" correct as we sang along with our favorite characters, the gorillas, as they trashed the camp. My mom sat in her rocking chair, chuckling as she took it all in. We laughed and enjoyed the time around the television.

Our TV habits began to change when I started high school. We finally had cable TV in the living room, first as a free trial to watch the summer Olympics and later when Major League Baseball moved all their games to cable networks. My mom was able to watch her beloved Cleveland baseball team without missing an at-bat. On the other hand, my dad discovered channels upon channels of shows he hadn't watched in years, maybe decades. There were also the weekends or holidays when premium channels were free. The western channel became my dad's favorite, and in those early years of cable TV in our house, many holidays were marked by hours and hours of cowboys, wagon trains, and John Wayne marathons, all in black and white.

This was also the time when the hours in my day were quickly consumed by other pursuits: school, homework, band, sports, clubs, dates. An increasingly busy schedule left little time for watching TV. My newly diagnosed migraines made, and still make, some movies and TV shows impossible to watch. I felt my symptoms build as my dad watched *Pearl Harbor* first on DVD and then on television. The planes swooped and dove and flew around the attack on the military base. It wasn't because I didn't want to watch the movie. I couldn't watch some of the same things my dad did because they made me physically sick. No matter how I explained it, he never believed me.

■ ■ ■

On a Wednesday afternoon in mid-July 2018, the summer before my dad retired, someone finally undid all my dad's work to prevent any air from moving around the house. We turned on the fans, opened the windows. We propped open solid exterior doors so the screens would allow fresh air into our home. Meanwhile, my dad tuned into *The Andy Griffith Show*. "I bet Andy Griffith makes some bucks off uh this show," my dad said. "It's on all the time!"

"Are you sure he's even still alive? This show's been in reruns for a while," my mom asked.

My dad looked shocked. "Aw, he can't be that old!" His voice showed his disbelief, that anyone would even think that Andy Griffith, whose shows were overwhelmingly filmed in black and white, could be dead. After all, my dad still held years-old aspirations of adopting a basset hound, naming it Goober after Goober Pyle (played by George Lindsey,) and letting it patrol the neighborhood until my dad yelled, "Hey, Goob!" to call the dog home. To me, my dad's plans neglected to acknowledge that my parents did not live in a town that even remotely resembled Mayberry. Their neighbors at the time all owned at least one shotgun and regularly had target practice in their yards. Roadkill was a normal occurrence, so normal that most of it went unnoticed. Coyotes prowled regularly.

Goober would not patrol for long.

My sister Katie joined my mom in getting to the root of Andy Griffith's place among the living. She pulled out her phone, did a quick search, and shared her findings. "Daddy, the entire cast of the show is dead."

Katie was almost right. One of the last members of the cast of *The Andy Griffith Show*, which went off the air in 1968 after running for eight seasons, died in 2012. Ron Howard, who played Opie, and a few supporting cast members were still alive with Howard being the youngest of the remaining cast.

My dad said nothing and turned away to face the television. His face was blank and stoic. A comforter with washing machine-faded clouds and Oreo cookies covered his legs despite the unbearable heat and humidity. If one didn't know better, he was just staring off into space.

We continued watching the ghosts as Andy, his son Opie, and his deputy Barney figured out what to do with the stray dogs that kept finding their way into the sheriff's station. Andy and Barney also tried to scrounge up the money needed to replace the cot in the town drunk's jail cell of choice, the place where he went to sober up before going home. I wondered what my dad thought as he sat there and watched. What kept his attention? Why did he tune in to these shows hour after hour, day after day? What did he see in these worlds full of ghosts that he couldn't find in the world he lives in? I wondered one more thing. I wanted to know what happens in my dad's head when he realizes just how many of the people he watches every day are dead.

■ ■ ■

There's nothing wrong with nostalgia, with looking back to parts of our past and basking in the familiar glow of what once was. I do it myself. I check my memories on Facebook almost daily. I sort through lanyards and name badges from years of camps and conferences, recalling the people I met, the friendships I formed, and the memories I made. There are things I refuse to let go of, special shelves filled with select books and trinkets. I stow important treasures, like the scarf my maternal grandmother wore after getting her hair done, in places I share with no one. The writer in me sees deep dives into nostalgia and the past as something essential to living in the world of the present. To understand the now, I also have to know the then.

Fine lines exist between nostalgia and withdrawing from the world. The key to all of this is knowing where those lines exist and knowing when enough is enough. Those boundaries are different for everyone and, more often than not, also rely on context. A person's relationship to the past is much too complicated to contain in a couple of paragraphs.

When I think about my dad and his TV, I wonder about these lines. My dad has withdrawn from most of the world. His circadian rhythm is almost gone. He has no idea what a loaf of bread costs. In his withdrawal from most of the world, he and his television have brought about other retreats. Katie barely leaves her bedroom after she comes home from work; she says that the living room has become "his space" where she doesn't feel welcome. My mom and Katie do all the work of maintaining the house. My dad is so out of shape from sitting in front of the television that walking the twenty feet from the bathroom to his recliner leaves him winded.

My dad has withdrawn from most of the world. His circadian rhythm is almost gone. He has no idea what a loaf of bread costs. In his withdrawal from most of the world, he and his television have brought about other retreats.

My visits home grow shorter and shorter. I want to spend time with people. I don't want to spend hours every day watching ghosts act out the same stories we saw the previous hour, the previous morning, week, year. On one such visit, my dad sat closer to the edge of his recliner. He hadn't been awake long. "You know, when I retired, I had a goal of living longer than my dad. I did it. Now my goal is to live longer than my mom," he said. His mom lived into her mid-eighties. My dad, who was in his late sixties at that time, had never planned to live as long as he has. Family history was not in his favor.

His goal is a good goal. But I wonder what my dad's life will look like if nothing changed but his age. If most of his life is spent retreating into television shows rooted in an increasingly distant past, then what does his retreat do to the present? The future?

■ ■ ■

Gunsmoke. Wagon Train. The Real McCoys. The Beverly Hillbillies. Bonanza. The Andy Griffith Show. Movies that appeared in theaters before my dad was born. Black and white ghosts parade across my parents' television screen for most of the hours in a day. Day after day after day.

Some days, my dad turns on these shows before the sun rises. Except for an hour when he watches a game show, he can spend all day in black and white, only returning to color for the six o'clock local news.

In the winter months, my dad can spend more hours with the ghosts than there are hours of daylight.

■ ■ ■

As I write this essay, I realize that I, too, am guilty of romanticizing the past. I've tuned out all the silent childhood dinners during the years when we had a television in the kitchen, when my dad told my sisters and I to be quiet because the news was on.

I've tuned out all the times in which my dad became visibly angry because of what someone else was watching. "What is this crap?" he seethed at the sight of *Say Yes to the Dress.* His next move before sticking out his hand and silently demanding the remote depended on his mood. Sometimes he grumbled comments about what he thought of the male fashion designer Randy's behavior, made assumptions about Randy's sexuality, and huffed that he didn't think "people like that" should be on TV. Other times, he wondered out loud why we even watched shows about pretty white dresses when we were going to get married wearing burlap sacks in our back yard.

I've tuned out the fact that the reason my sisters and I could watch cartoons on Saturdays without someone changing the channel was because my dad was at work.

I've tuned out how many hours my sisters and I spent in our childhood bedrooms to avoid the television, despite having sets in our rooms. Has the living room ever been a family space?

I've tuned out a lot of these televised memories because the past has bled into the present. The past is not a place where I want to spend the rest of my days. The past hurts, but it helps me understand until I realize that I still can't wrap my head around any of this.

■ ■ ■

I worry about the past. I wonder what will happen when my dad's choices in TV run out of history to regress to. What happens when he gets so far back in time that there is no more TV to watch? What happens when he stays rooted so far in the past that there's nothing to connect him to the present?

■ ■ ■

During more than one visit home after my dad retired, I tried to understand why he continued to watch these ghosts. The same ghosts. I wanted to know what he looked for in these shows that I have yet to find. At one point early in his retirement, he figured out how to fill his days with nothing but *Gunsmoke* while only changing the channel twice. For the past few years, the television watched him sleep more than he watched the television.

On more than one occasion, I made myself watch these shows. Hours of *Gunsmoke* until I worried that the opening music was etched so deep in my brain that those chords would be impossible to forget. I tried to find something, a clue, as to why my dad kept watching. As far as obvious clues go, I found nothing.

As I tried to watch *Gunsmoke* and the other shows my dad watched every day, I wondered what kept him so enthralled. Is it because of what my dad called "good stories?" I don't know. For me, it didn't take long before the plots of each episode started to become one and the same. We started at the saloon, the peace was disturbed, and by the end of the episode, justice was served and order restored. If this is what my dad thinks is a good story, then the writer in me wants to know what we sacrifice so that this level of repetition becomes the hallmark of good stories.

But I don't think that is what happens when my dad turns on the TV. Maybe it's what these shows represent and that holds my dad's attention. A certain kind of clear and well-defined masculinity, a precise line between good and evil, tales of adventure. A particular kind of America that I never lived in or identified with. The more I force myself to watch and analyze, the more I realize that this is a particular kind of nostalgia with which I cannot reconcile. Worlds have changed. The lines between differences were never as clear as they are in these worlds of the television screen. Women aren't the little ladies looking for a husband, a savior, or a home to keep. The local U.S. marshal isn't going to maintain law and order simply because he has a badge and a gun.

My dad slips further and further into his shows as I try to understand. At one point, he regularly spoke like Festus Haggen (played by Ken Curtis), a distinctive twang weaving in and out of his speech patterns. "Aw I'm just teasin' yuh," he said when I brought this observation up. "What's your maw got planned for dinner? I sure am fixin' for some vittles."

"I hate when he calls me maw," my mom said when my dad was out of earshot. "I am his wife, not his mother."

Sometimes I rolled my eyes when my dad spoke like Festus. Sometimes I sighed loud enough to catch his attention. I tried everything from pointing out the obvious—"You sound like Festus on *Gunsmoke*"—to an academic explanation of what my dad calls "talkin' hillbilly" really is. More and more, I don't try to keep the peace. On one occasion, he dismissed me with a guttural "eh!" On another, he commented that "all that school made you forget how to take a joke."

On yet another occasion, I attempted an analysis of Festus's character after my dad commented about Festus's ability to talk out both sides of his mouth. I launched into a commentary about the Greek god who I presumed Festus was named after and that god's story. I tied in feminist theory. I was quite literally pulling my thoughts out of my ass, but to me, it made sense. I thought this might be the way I found something that captured my interest in the shows my dad spent his days immersed in.

"You really do know how to suck the fun out everything, don't ya?" he said without making eye contact.

I did not take the fun out of his shows. I just asked him to occasionally be present in a world that doesn't revolve around TV screens, ghosts projected in black and white, and the remote control.

■ ■ ■

I worry about the present. My dad rarely leaves the house anymore except for his daily trip to McDonald's for a large iced coffee. Twelve miles round trip. Sugar-free vanilla syrup, extra cream, has a code from the app. Against the advice of more than one of his doctors from the VA. Contrary to the fact that he has never liked coffee. Instead of a hobby or calling someone up for a chat, it's *Gunsmoke. Bonanza. The Andy Griffith Show.* Black and white movies. Something, anything, to remove himself from the present and place him in the past, a time in which he says he wasn't happy either. I wonder if his attempts to drown out the world around him are successful. I wonder if what he finds in his "good stories" makes him feel... something. Entertained? Comfortable? Secure?

Whatever it is that he looks for, he finds more and more of it in the ghosts on TV and less and less in the living people who surround him. When prompted, he claims he doesn't remember: birthdays, holidays, details of weddings and graduations, the day of the week. But he always remembers what is on TV and what time the show will air.

■ ■ ■

Part of my want to understand what my dad finds in watching ghosts on TV is me not understanding television in the first place.

I am not a TV person. The idea of binge watching anything makes me shutter. My attention span shrinks drastically when I see a television screen come to life, so much so that I struggle to finish the shortest of movies without turning my focus to something else. My TV will spend hours, sometimes days, sitting in silence. I don't have shows with new episodes or season premieres to change my schedule. Shoot, I don't even have cable. If I'm watching television, I watch and do something else. Watch and read. Watch and clean. Watch and grade. On the rare occasion that all my attention is dedicated to what is on the television screen, then the events unfolding in my living room must be monumental.

This aversion to television has to come from somewhere. It isn't hard for me to list the reasons that compel me not to watch TV. The constant sound is overwhelming. My hands need something to do. My mind struggles to turn off the internal monologue that lists what I want or need to do. Sometimes, I just don't find a show that captures my attention. Instead, I turn on music or simply go about my day with the TV at rest. Other times, I'll turn on Food Network or another channel where people do seemingly normal, everyday things, but I use those shows as background noise when I don't want to be alone with my thoughts.

What I want to dig into is not what I find off putting about TV, but what the root cause is and how I arrived somewhere so very different from my dad. If I am completely honest with myself, I wonder how much of this aversion is a trauma response. Having someone repeatedly tell you that your

What I want to dig into is not what I find off putting about TV, but what the root cause is and how I arrived somewhere so very different from my dad.

choices are wrong, that what you like is wrong, and that you as someone's child are not their priority likely does something to a person's mentality, and I wonder what it has done to mine. When I dig any deeper, though, my mind freezes until thoughts come to me at random times, like just as I'm heading out the door on a Sunday afternoon to meet friends for our weekly coffee and writing time. This aversion may not be to television itself, but to the "good stories" that these choices in television perpetuate. In those stories, those worlds that my dad routinely immerses himself in, I am not present. My sisters are not present; neither is my mom. There are no responsibilities that my dad is held accountable for. There aren't differences of opinion he needs navigate, questions that he must answer, or challenges he will face. He can just be.

The root cause of this aversion could be that the world full of what my dad considers "good stories" is a world in which nothing is real but himself. It is a world where I am not wanted or needed by a person who is fifty percent responsible for me existing in this world. In the world of these "good stories," everything does revolve around my dad because in that tiny microcosm of existence, he holds a level of control that is non-negotiable and above all others—whatever he says via an unspoken language of pressing buttons on the remote is the unquestioned law. If he doesn't like what's happening or the narrative gets difficult to digest, he can simply end the sequence of events by pressing the power button. He doesn't have to answer to doctors if he doesn't want to. He doesn't have to hear me talking about my students' goofy antics in class or the latest news of police brutality or civil rights. He doesn't have to think when he is in the world of the "good stories" on television.

That kind of power does not exist outside of the box of black and white ghosts that is the television, and it is certainly not a kind of power that he can ethically exercise over my mom nor logistically use to control three headstrong, independent daughters. In some ways, the "good stories" of the television ghosts aren't the stories that the shows' producers crafted, but the world my dad has constructed around the cowboys, the wagon trains, and the "good stories." I wish I could dig deeper, down to the nucleus of what has happened and will continue to happen, to understand what it is that makes my dad claim he is so utterly unhappy that this is the only solace he can find. There is something hidden in my memories that would help me find what I want to understand, but that channel is not currently a part of my subscription package.

■ ■ ■

I worry about him, my dad. I worry about the future.

I know my dad's viewing habits are not going to change. He is stubborn and set in his ways. His ghosts are on loop, day after day, acting out the same stories. He sleeps through more and more of these shows. There is little I can do to break his cycle of moving farther back in time while the rest of my family moves forward. I have tried. My sisters have tried. My mom has tried.

As time goes on, I watch what my dad's television choices do to our family. There are no breaks for holidays or visits from friends or family. He ignores or gets aggressively angry if someone asks him to turn the TV off or to simply turn down the volume. Katie doesn't spend time in the living room, or really the first floor of the house. There are evenings when my mom has given up watching the news or the baseball game because my dad can't miss what is most likely a rerun of one of his shows. My dad regularly forgets that I have seen these shows and ghosts before, asking if I've heard of or watched this show multiple times in one visit home. He once asked me on the phone if I had been keeping up with *Gunsmoke*, as if a new season had just started.

Those repeated questions make me wonder just what my dad will remember in the future. "I can't remember anything these days," is a common reason my dad offers when he forgets what day it is, who is in the house, or even after the second, third, or fourth time he asks what's for dinner. He blames his forgetfulness on a variety of things: an accident at work before he retired, medical incidents for which batteries of tests come back inconclusive, drinking Diet Coke, not caring about other people because retirement is all about him. None of these things are somehow his fault but I cannot remove his TV habits from these equations.

Ultimately, I wonder what will happen when my dad runs out of ghosts to watch. I fear there will be a time when I come home and find him sitting in the same brown recliner where he has sat for years. Eyes focused on the television screen, blank look on his face. His arms and arthritic hands rest perfectly still and straight on the arm rests of his chair. The footrest is fully extended. A blanket covers his legs. When I walk into the room, he doesn't say my name in triplicate—"Ashley Ashley Ashley!"— like he does every single time I cross his line of vision.

This time, though, the television screen is as blank as the expression on his face. I wonder what he'll say if I ask what he's watching, if he will say anything at all. In this moment somewhere in the future, not only has my dad gone so far into the past that he has lost recognition of the present, but has gone somewhere where even the ghosts can't be seen on TV anymore. ■

PISTIS

Tonight, wind and the bottle drag him up from sweaty bed
to sit outside and let them both go to work on his mind.
There are things he dreams but can't pronounce and still
would choose in lieu of pride or money: a hand placed just so
and sturdy in the small of his back, frozen toes but tingling
towards a stove faithfully tended, one single reason to use
or sell the lapis-beaded rosary. The night wind moves him
and he's finally come to the edge. He can see the seams.
Like a finch after first flight, there's finally some perspective
on the nest. When they turn up and find him cold as morning
they'll keep saying what a waste, what a goddamn shame.

GARRETT STACK

CAR SHOW

It's evening down at the Legion
and the old men have their hoods up
to say *I've got nothing
to hide.* Everyone's happy leaning against
their private vision of perfection
and everyone's sad it took this long
to acquire. But here they are now
sore backed and heart burnt,
tattoos all faded like the name of the girl
who turned up her nose at the rusted
truck and *Goddamn if only
she could see me now.*
When they lean over another man's engine
they'll compliment his cams, the line
of his straight six, the distant thunder
as he sits young again, strong
limbed and staring at his old hometown
trying to decide if someday
he will buy it all up
or burn it all down.

GARRETT STACK

MANNEQUIN BLUE

Black frost. Silver thaw.
The light hesitates for its own good.
When airy pastures lead to crowded
cliffs, an alarm clock stutters off
the nightstand, minutes all the same,
generations flicker on the dotted
wallpaper, and why wonder, how
did we get here? She left the Tempo
idling in Roswell. Wipers waving
on a cloudless holiday. But this is not
a dream as it should be. Though
the ache is real, in lucid gloom,
a little groggy on the comedown.
She comes back—steam hissing
like a factory stampede, ironing her
fists by the motel window. It's a tight rope.
Drenched in the overwhelm, she feels
for parallel stitches, unthreads miles
of twine from her knuckles, loosens
every last pin and flings them to the ice
bowl. Prettier than the bride, she trips
on the train of her mannequin who
straddles a chair with its head spinning
round like a globe. She cuffs. She throws.
She tailors her spine, her pulse drums
louder than oceans uncorked to cover
tomorrow's ruins. To be seen in less
is to be hollow is to be true.

Violet moths. White amnesia.
A foghorn blares for sleepwalkers

as she drifts in a nightgown in a town
she can't pronounce, chasing her
mother's dress made of charcoal.
If we were formed by friction,
from silk and scraping rocks,
then her cheeks should be sharp
enough to cut through boarded
buildings before she erodes like
the contours of a glacier.
But she doesn't know her way yet
with sparks, how stiletto earthquakes
can uproot a graveyard if the keeper's
on strike for more than a service, when
they fail to bait the mouse traps on
mausoleum floors. The gate's wide open.
She only wears lipstick to funerals,
the ones where a phone rings in a robe
throughout the benediction, where she's
reminded of towels in the dryer,
the humdrum rumbling *déjà vu*,
the need to flatten geography, how
brief the geometry of a snowflake.

CHAD WEEDEN

SUBDIVISIONS

How many hawks above the demolition?
Soot-coated like the moon, circling the stench
of what remains when we divide: Arabella
Bridge, your abyss, a pair of bloodhounds
roped to the welcome sign, hunched
and fevered, ready to charge a right of passage
out of range. They say it's controlled. That it's
dire, life's benign repetition, until it's not.
But so's the course. Like longevity's flawed
arithmetic—if I don't see you here, I'll see
you there, new monotony, on the edge
of Gypsy Park, where we'd sit for an hour
every other Tuesday on a bus stop bench
as the kudzu giants absorbed the subdivision.
I'd arrive early. Disarmed the moment
to scrub the rows of tabloid foliage, sizing
the obituaries for palpitations and a role model
of the atomic age. I wasn't waving at you, he'd say,
I was blocking the sun. Eyes glossy and green,
he'd dull the light if it was harsh. Which is why
he was always late, by routine, blank like attic
manuscripts, zippo-flicking through bleary phantasms
of a woman scaling fish on a beach, his brother
yelling from a dune, or the prescriptions forgot,
always patting his breast pocket for that full rattle
of capsules I doubt he strained his exhalations
on purpose. We'd crouch and cover. Wrapped in vines
like who will cut our passage from the overgrowth
to the cradle thats rocks against the tremors enough
to inch our asylum from creases in a milestone.

CHAD WEEDEN

BOOK REVIEW

Kelly McQuain. *Scrape the Velvet From Your Antlers.*
Huntsville, Tex.: Texas Review Press, 2023. 83 pages.
Softcover. $21.95.

Reviewed by Jacob Strautmann

Kelly McQuain's *Scrape the Velvet
From Your Antlers*, composed in
part from his two earlier chapbooks,
Velvet Rodeo and *Antlers*, was chosen
as the West Virginia selection for the
TRP Southern Poetry Breakthrough
Prize, and—kudos to the Texas
Review Press—they have chosen a
book unlimited by regional concern
or scope and an author whose poems
sing. In "Glass Frog," the poet begins
in describing the translucent skin of a species of frog in
Central America, before speculating, by way of an anatomy
kit the poet played with as child, what human beings would
perceive had we this same feature:

  .... The fat

  around viscera; meat

slow to digest in a stomach that sits inches
beneath a glass-

stripped of symbolism to mechanical beat?

McQuain's answer? "I'd like to think / we'd find
eloquence…" In this movement—from nature's oddity to the
displayed human body, and from youth into empathy and
hope for humanity, McQuain sketches the outline of this first
and memorable collection of poetry.

These poems are rural and urban, self-aware and traveled.
For instance, McQuain, who was Allegheny-born and now
teaches in Philadelphia, visits the story of the the androgynous
bodhisattva Guanyin, known most for compassion, but in the
poem "Tonight Guanyin Seeks and End to Suffering" walking
the streets downtown:

This is how a young man
                      becomes a Mary

anything but virginal:
                      Guanyin

Strutting in stiletto heels
    beneath October street lamps, cutting

a slender silhouette   among headlights
sharking by.

And Guanyin's compassion isn't only reserved for the
transgendered or the prostitute. McQuain's Whitmanesque
gesture allows Guanyin to welcome all in from their suffering:

```
                ....In her arms
    she holds        mothers whose children

disappear,          fathers whose cars
    cruise city streets...
```

McQuain's use of the lacunae (or extra spaces between words), which here could indicate suffering caught in headlights as another car rounds the corner, and used often in McQuain's other poems as an open space allowing the reader to linger a little longer, come a little closer, is just one way his facility with the conventions of poetry connect meaning to form.

He most often does so by worrying the language. *Scrape the Velvet From Your Antlers* is about transformation, becoming, and belonging, and McQuain's callbacks in syllable and sound are breathtakingly apropos. In "Southern Heat," the poet inhabits his younger perspective, as he does often in this book, speaking from the backseat of a car in summer in Georgia—in a scene that would be right at home in Flannery O'Connor's "A Good Man Is Hard to Find"—and points at a boy and girl with cornrows sitting on a stoop, asks innocently, "Who're they?" And hears his preacher-in-training grandfather, called "Grandpop" here, say the n-word, his first time encountering the slur: "Hot wind/ through the window wouldn't blow it away."

The sensitive speaker, only seven, but aware of the power of hate-speech, blames himself: "I am the one who'd made him say / the Word..." And we see that internalization of blame take place: "Difference burned, too..." "...hot Georgia dust clawed at my throat..." "...the hot vinyl seat / burning me. I was burning alive! / Damn if I didn't hate everyone / the way

I hated myself inside." But even in quenching his raw throat, the speaker takes in the blame further, drinks it in, through internal rhyme (italics mine):

...I begged Mama for a grape pop.
She hunted for coins as Grandpop strode in
To shoot the shit with the storekeeper.

And because McQuain has so deftly laid the groundwork, the reader can't help but see the echo of the word grandfather spoke in the grape Nehi the boy holds to his chest as it burns.

Despite his fire and brimstone grandfather, the proximity of the land to the poet's imagination means another god oversees this book and the transformations at its heart. In the title poem, which appears early in the volume, as his siblings head for the horizon, the poet has other preoccupations: "As you take the hill, the hill takes you." He keeps his head down as he walks through cockleburs and lashing grasses, asking "Who fiddled with you—rewired deference / into difference?" Unlike the "Southern Heat" poem, in this one the child's perspective is supplanted again and again by the gay man he would become. Looking into the pine shade, he asks:

What kneels to drink in that dark?
What hooved thing—some player
of panpipes moving? A preacher
might call this moment choosing.

Ultimately, the poet decides "Something calls you somewhere else." West Virginia and his readers are lucky McQuain took so much with him. ∎

I WILL BE A TERRIBLE WIDOW

Paint your name in blue
on my cathedral heart.
When they crack me open,
I want them to know
how much you loved me.
Brave this place a little longer.
Brave this air just for me.
Press your teeth along my neck,
and give me salt when
I ask for water. You
are the steady stone
who keeps safe the paper.
What comfort I know dwells
in your calloused hands.
If you leave: taillights and dust,
a hollow where you used to sit
with nothing strong enough
to lift your chin but
the soft flush of my hair
pressed to your cheek.
I'll wander lost, a map
without a country.
For all the black I own
and all the fire I carry, the red
that tethers me to earth
is you.

ANN DeVILBISS

A MORE TENDER AIM

A doe with glammy eyes
high steps through the yard
toward the remains
of an eviscerated pumpkin
abandoned in the pachysandra

From behind the door, I see her
and recognize the hunger
for more than a few green
leaves still clinging to trees
in a seedy world full of orange

CJ FARNSWORTH

CONTRIBUTORS

Ashley Anderson's work has appeared in or is forthcoming from *Newfound, Hobart, Assay: A Journal of Nonfiction Studies, Wraparound South, Permafrost, Cosmonauts Avenue, Tahoma Literary Review, Badlands Literary Journal, Quarter After Eight,* and others. She holds a PhD in English with a creative writing emphasis from the University of Missouri and MA degrees from Kent State University and the University of Cincinnati. Anderson currently teaches first-year composition with some Taylor Swift mixed in at the University of Missouri and, when she isn't writing or teaching, can be found making something she found somewhere online.

Artist, poet, and curator **John Brooks**'s visual work has been exhibited in the United States and Europe and is held in the collections of 21C Museum Hotels, Grinnell College Museum of Art, OZ Arts, The University of Kentucky Medical Center, and numerous private collections; he has been featured in *The New Yorker, The Yale Review, Action Spectacle,* and *Golf Digest.* In 2022, he had solo exhibitions at MAARCH in New York City and Luis De Jesus Los Angeles. Brooks's poetry has been published in *Good River Review, Assaracus, East by Northeast,* and *Plainsongs,* and he has written criticism for *Ruckus Journal, UnderMain, BOMB,* and *Strange Fire Collective.* From 2017-2022, Brooks operated Quappi Projects, a Louisville-based contemporary art gallery focusing on exhibiting work reflective of the zeitgeist, where he curated over twenty-five exhibitions. He is also the chairperson of Sarabande Books' Board of Directors.

Ann DeVilbiss (she/her) has work published or forthcoming in *Columbia Journal, Gertrude, The Maine Review, Painted Bride Quarterly, Radar,* and elsewhere. She has received support from the Kentucky Arts Council and the Kentucky Foundation for Women, and she lives and works in Louisville, Kentucky.

Ansel Elkins is the author of *Blue Yodel,* winner of the 2014 Yale Series of Younger Poets Prize. She has received fellowships from the National Endowment for the Arts, the North Carolina Arts

Council, the American Antiquarian Society, and Bread Loaf Writers' Conference, as well as a Discovery/*Boston Review* Prize. She's currently a visiting creative writing professor at Berea College.

CJ Farnsworth is a poet residing in West Virginia and is a graduate of Vermont College of Fine Arts. Her poems have appeared or are forthcoming in *I-70 Review, Bluestone Review, IMPOST, Kenning, Kestrel, Rattle, Women Speak,* and others. She is a Pushcart Prize nominee. Her first full-length poetry collection was published by Sheila-Na-Gig in fall 2023.

Poet, writer, editor, **Tamara J. Madison**, is the author of *Threed, This Road Not Damascus* (Trio House Press); *Kentucky Curdled and Sistuh's Sermon on the Mount* (all poetry), and *Collard County* (fiction). Her writing is inspired by her ancestry and relations. She is the creator of *BREAKDOWN: The Poet & The Poems,* a YouTube conversation series promoting poets and their poetry as inspiration for everyday life. Madison has also shared her poetry on the TEDx platform. She is a MFA graduate of New England College and an Anaphora Arts Fellow (2021). She currently teaches English and Creative Writing in central Florida.

Mindy Misener grew up in Maine and is a graduate of Williams College and the University of Michigan. Her stories and essays have appeared or are forthcoming in *The Common, The Pinch, Image,* and *CrossCurrents.* She lives with her family in Bozeman, Montana, and teaches creative writing at Montana State University.

Lindsey Pharr lives and writes outside of Asheville, North Carolina. Her work has appeared in *SmokeLong Quarterly, River Teeth, Longleaf Review,* and elsewhere. She is currently pursuing an MFA in Creative Nonfiction at the Naslund-Mann Graduate School of Writing at Spalding University in Louisville, Kentucky.

Garrett Stack's first book is *Yeoman's Work* (Bottom Dog Press, 2020) which contains two Pushcart Nominees. His poems were most recently published in *Tar River, Atlanta Review,* and *Third Wednesday.* He edits the *Lakeshore Review* and teaches at Ferris State University in West Michigan.

Raised in Marshall County, West Virginia., **Jacob Strautmann** is a recipient of the Massachusetts Poetry Fellowship from the Massachusetts Cultural Council. His poems have appeared in the *Boston Globe, Agni Magazine, Salamander Magazine, Southern Humanities Review, Blackbird,* and other publications. He is an Associate Director of Development Communications at Boston University, where he also teaches playwriting. He lives in Greater Boston with his partner Valerie Duff and their two children. Strautmann is currently at work on a third manuscript of poems, which is a painting-poetry collaboration with the German artist Eva Strautmann. It is tentatively titled *Abstractions.*

Chad Weeden's work has appeared in *Jet Fuel Review, Asheville Poetry Review, Crosswinds Poetry Journal, Pedestal Magazine, great weather for MEDIA, Iodine Poetry Journal, Main Street Rag* & the *Kakalak.* He lives in Newport, Rhode Island.

Kate Wright grew up in the northern Appalachians, where she received her BA and MA in English from Penn State. She is currently a PhD student at the University of Tennessee, where she serves as the poetry editor of *Grist.* Her work has appeared in or is forthcoming from *Rogue Agent, Okay Donkey, The Maine Review, Ghost City Press,* and elsewhere. You can find her on Twitter @KateWrightPoet

www.ingramcontent.com/pod-product-compliance
Lightning Source LLC
Chambersburg PA
CBHW070604180626
46817CB00005B/1996